WE REFUSE TO STARVE IN SILENCE

We Refuse to Starve in Silence

A History of the National Unemployed Workers' Movement, 1920-46

RICHARD CROUCHER

LAWRENCE AND WISHART
LONDON

Lawrence and Wishart Limited
39 Museum Street
London WC1A 1LQ

First published 1987

Photoset in North Wales by
Derek Doyle & Associates, Mold, Clwyd
Printed and bound in Great Britain by
The Camelot Press, Southampton

Contents

Illustrations

All photographs courtesy Communist Party Picture Library, except demonstrators at Stepney Labour Exchange, courtesy Christopher Brunel

Preface

This book is the result of a collective effort. Many people contributed material and ideas to it, including numerous old members of the unemployed movement. Many of these contributions are acknowledged in the footnotes, but I would especially like to thank Vic Graves, Liz Lane, Doug Low, Derick Newland, Sheila Saunders, Keith Jerrome and Terry Burgess for putting themselves out to help me. Claus Scharf of the Institut für Europäische Geschichte, Mainz and Richard Storey of the Modern Records Centre, University of Warwick, responded to regular requests for help. I hope that they, and all those whom I have not mentioned, find this book sufficiently useful to justify the effort which they made.

Wolverton, September 1986

Sources

The two principal archival sources for this book were the Library of the Communist Party and the Marx Memorial Library. The majority of internal NUW(C)M circulars are to be found in the former, whilst the Conference and NAC Reports are in the latter. Hannington's personal collection of documents has been divided between the two libraries; in addition, Maud Brown's papers are in the Marx Memorial Library. Since these documents played such a large part in researching this book, they are referred to in footnotes as WH/CP and WH/MML. File numbers are given where they could be attributed. Government files in the Public Record Office are given their PRO reference together with the date of the document, e.g. 24 January 1922. CAB 24/1288.

Interviews have been conducted by the author unless otherwise indicated; the tapes are in my possession.

Introduction

The history of the National Unemployed Workers' Movement (NUWM) is central to British history between the wars. The NUWM's tireless campaigns on behalf of the unwaged and dispossessed mobilised hundreds of thousands of people in battles on behalf of the millions who were victims of the long inter-war slump. The NUWM played an important part in protecting the position of those in work as well as those out of work, by preventing mass strike-breaking in industrial disputes. Although it was not unique in international labour history as a campaigning organisation of unemployed, it did have many distinctive characteristics and represented a highpoint of unemployed organisation in British history. Its origins, development, internal life, external relations and politics are particularly relevant to the trade union movement today, when unemployment has again become a major scourge. This is the justification for a history of the NUWM as an organisation, at a time when this type of history is distinctly unfashionable.

The work of the NUWM is not unknown, even if much of its internal history remains obscure. Generations of activists have been reared on Wal Hannington's accounts, especially on his racy and inspiring *Unemployed Struggles*. Hannington, the movement's leader throughout its life, wrote a series of influential works which dominate existing perceptions of the NUWM. Joan Smith also collaborated with Hannington's Scottish right-hand man, Harry McShane, to tell McShane's story in *No Mean Fighter*. But the accounts given by the movement's leaders have to be closely interrogated when they speak of history. Peter Kingsford began this process with his interesting history *The Hunger Marchers in Britain*. Yet we are still left with an impression of the organisation as a march

organising and support movement. This book therefore tries
to look critically at the existing literature, whilst following a
narrative which focuses on the NUWM's non-marching
activities. It is designed to be read in conjunction with these
other books: no attempt is made to repeat what is said in them
except in so far as is necessary.

The pages which follow examine the history of the NUWM,
and particularly its external relations with other labour
movement bodies. Any history of the NUWM which isolated
it from its labour movement context would be seriously
deficient because of the importance of external support for any
unemployed organisation. Relations with the Communist and
Labour Parties, with the trade unions and other unemployed
movements, are therefore treated seriously both for compara-
tive and explanatory reasons. There is a sense, then, in which
this book looks outwards as much as inwards; since this
orientation was shared by unemployed activists of the years
being studied, it is felt to be a perspective worth adopting.

The history of the NUWM is traced in the briefest, and, it is
hoped, therefore most accessible way. But such a short
treatment cannot possibly do full justice to such a lively
organisation with so many active branches. The evidence of
their varied and imaginative work is present in the records left
by Wal Hannington, on which this book is largely based. Yet
it has been impossible to present this in all its breadth whilst
keeping the manuscript under control. A presentation of the
history of the NUWM which fully reflected the diversity of its
work would be a multi-volume study. One of the merits of a
study on this scale would be that it would give an opportunity
for the author to acknowledge the efforts of so many
individual activists who built and sustained the NUWM; such
a study would be a useful if major task for an historian to
undertake. Meanwhile, it is hoped that this book will provide
some sort of inadequate monument to their dedication and
self-sacrifice; it is certainly offered in a spirit of solidarity with
those people.

1

Unemployment and the System of Relief Between the Wars

The end of the First World War brought a brief boom. It was not to last. During the winter of 1920-21, the number of people out of work grew rapidly and reached 1,500,000 by the spring. By July 1921, over 2,000,000 people had been thrown on to an inadequate system of poor relief. The number of people recognised by official statisticians as being unemployed was not to fall below 1,000,000 for the rest of the decade, and the 1920s closed with the figure rising steadily towards 2,000,000. The next three years were to be even worse, with some 3,000,000 officially unemployed in the depths of the world Depression. But even before those years, the level of unemployment had been on an historical plateau; such consistently high figures were much worse than for the first two decades of the century.[1] Coming after the full employment of the First World War, the shock was especially severe.

The number of people who were unemployed at one time or another was very much greater than the bald statistics suggest. The 'scrap heap' analogy is misleading here: it would be more helpful to imagine a river with people joining and leaving like rainfall and evaporation. Sidney Pollard has estimated that in the depths of the world Depression, the total number of people *touched* personally by unemployment amounted to about half of the British workforce.[2] Many of those affected were unemployed for only a relatively short period of time; nevertheless, they could not themselves predict the length of their unemployment. Being out of work was an experience common to a large part of the British working class in the inter-war years. Not only was there no clear dividing line between the employed and the unemployed, as people drifted in and out of work, there was also a great deal of overlap between these two 'sections' of the working class. Short periods of notice and no redundancy payments made descent into poverty a very immediate and tangible threat to those in work. Fear of the descent and sympathy for those already at the bottom of the slope were the consequences among the employed. Conversely, few of the unemployed saw their position as permanent, except in certain particularly bad localities.

If the boundary between those in and out of work makes it difficult to estimate the real impact of worklessness, government statistics compound the problem. Their silences conceal a great deal, and the published figures do not even give an accurate 'photographic' reflection of the numbers affected at any one time. The figures related only to insured workers, and therefore excluded agricultural, council and certain types of railway workers. Informed commentators by no means hostile to the government estimated in 1922 that the figures should be revised upwards by somewhere between 11.9 and 13.8 per cent to take account of this factor alone. The academics in question also drew attention to the importance of short-time working, and suggested a further 7-9 per cent increase for this reason. Finally, there was the even more important issue of unregistered unemployment among those for whom, like many married women, there was no financial benefit in signing on but who would have welcomed work. Their number is very difficult to estimate, but could have been as large as the number of men registered as unemployed.[3] Taken as a whole, these considerations allow us to say that the official figures could probably on occasion have been doubled to give the true number of those seeking work and unable to find it.

The majority of the registered unemployed in the inter-war years were manual workers in the staple industries. During the 1920s, white-collar workers remained a relatively secure section of the workforce. Workers in the textile, steel, shipbuilding and coalmining industries were the main victims of the economic situation. In mining, the advent of mass unemployment came relatively late (in 1927), but was particularly dramatic. Whole regions were laid waste by the sudden and deep decline in the coal industry. There were two important consequences of unemployment being concentrated in this sector of the economy, the main manufacturing and extractive industries. Firstly, because the industries were concentrated in certain areas, so, too, were the majority of the workless. Throughout the 1920s, nine counties with less than half of the insured population provided 70 per cent of the unemployed.[4] By the late 1920s, public perception of unemployment as a localised problem took root, encouraged by state policy. Governments actively highlighted this aspect of the situation, and put it at the centre of their approach. The transference of workers from the depressed areas to the more prosperous towns of the Midlands and South-East became an important plank in their policies.[5] The symptoms were being treated rather than the national disease. Secondly, the concentration of unemployment in the staple industries had important consequences for the possibilities of building an unemployed movement. The overwhelming majority of the workless had some experience of the disciplines, routines and benefits of collective organisation through their trade unions, and felt the need to bring this experience to bear when they fell out of work. The traditions of union organisation were strongest in the skilled sector of the workforce, but between the wars these workers lost their traditionally sheltered position. The Amalgamated Engineering Union (AEU), almost exclusively a skilled men's union, never had less than 8 per cent of its members out of work between 1922 and 1935. The shipbuilding unions were even harder hit. In the depths of the world Depression, the Boilermakers' Society had a phenomenal 60 per cent of its members unemployed, with devastating effects on its finances.[6] The skilled workers in the staple industries were to play a crucial role in the leadership of the unemployed movement at national and local level. In many respects, that movement reflected their own unions with all their strengths and weaknesses.

However, the image of the typical unemployed person in the inter-war years as a male manual worker from heavy industry was, at least in part, a political construction. Large numbers of women had been employed in the munitions industries during the First World War, but they were unceremoniously removed from the official figures as early as February 1919, on the grounds that their normal work no longer existed.[7] Women who had worked in the engineering and munitions industries during the war were 're-classified' according to the trades that they had (or more commonly, had not) followed before 1914. The great majority of the 900,000 women who had worked in munitions were therefore eliminated, as most of them had not worked in one of the almost entirely male industries which had been part of the insurance scheme.[8] Yet many of these women wanted work. In early 1919, the National Federation of Women Workers launched a campaign to assert women's right to work ('Work, Not Doles' they demanded).[9] It was at this point that the question of who was to be legitimately described as unemployed was raised most sharply as a political problem. The Lloyd George government recognised this and undermined the campaign by appealing to local authorities to employ ex-servicemen in preference to women.[10] Women were being encouraged to accept a definition of themselves as having no right to paid employment. They became the largest and most 'invisible' part of the reserve army of labour.

The ex-servicemen generally supported this situation, seeing the women as having taken jobs which were rightfully theirs as 'breadwinners'. Some of the first unemployed struggles of the post-war period were in fact attempts by ex-servicemen to seize jobs filled by women; women tram conductors in Bristol had their trams attacked and pushed off the rails in 1919, for example. The political advantage was definitely with the ex-servicemen in this argument. Although by October 1919 they only constituted about one-third of the unemployed, their specific weight was politically very great. It was these men, and particularly the disabled among them, who loomed large in the popular image of the workless. People saw them as worthy of great sympathy. The unemployed were therefore easily able to justify militant protest against unemployment both to themselves and others. They were also very reluctant to agree to any broadening of the definition of the unemployed to include women, because they feared that this might dilute sympathy for them. During the 1920s, they were to set the tone of the unemployed movement. It was not until the 1930s, when the memory of the war was receding, that women were allowed to play a major part in the movement.

Poverty and the System of Relief

It was women who faced the intensification of domestic labour and grinding poverty associated with unemployment in these years. They were the hardest hit, often sacrificing their health to that of their menfolk and children. It was their experience above all which confirmed the fact that the majority of the unemployed and their families lived in absolute poverty between the wars. Despite attempts to show that this was not the case, the weight of medical opinion is also overwhelmingly on the side of this statement.[11] The link between poor housing, inadequate diets, shabby clothing, ill health and unemployment was proven to many people's satisfaction during the 1930s.

The reasons for mass poverty and ill health following directly from unemployment were unquestionably rooted in the utterly inadequate system of relief which existed in 1919. The unemployed movement had a good deal of historical space for its arguments, as it was widely recognised in governing circles that the system was in great need of extensive reform. Without this recognition, the unemployed movement could have been met by repression alone. As it was, the movement, along with the Labour Party and elements in the Liberal Party, was to engage in a long historical negotiation with the Conservatives about the nature of welfare provision.

In 1919, few were prepared to defend the existing system in its entirety. Most informed commentators accepted that it was quite inadequate for dealing with mass unemployment in the twentieth century. Basically the same structure that had been instituted, despite vigorous objections, in 1834, it was designed to deal with the small numbers driven by desperation to submit to its hardships and humiliations.

The 1834 Poor Law applied only in England and Wales. Its central principles were that no relief would be given to the able-bodied except through the workhouse; that this relief should bring a worse standard of life than that of the worst-off labourer outside and that men and women should be separated in the workhouse. The system was run by locally elected Boards of Guardians, whose main officials were Relieving Officers and the Workhouse Master. The Guardians derived their funds from local rates, and were thus pressurised to keep relief (and therefore rates) low. Claimants applied to the Guardians for help, and, initially on the decision of a Relieving Officer, were given either 'out-relief', part of which was to be given in kind, or accommodation in the workhouse. Workhouse regimes were generally very strict and a whole literature bears testimony to the inhuman and degrading treatment which many people experienced in the 'Bastilles'.

The whole system was already thought outmoded and inappropriate by the Royal Commission's 1909 report. Although there were majority and minority reports, there was unanimous agreement that the local Boards of Guardians should be abolished. It was generally felt that the system was inequitable and inconsistently administered by different Boards. But by this time, opponents of the system had already begun to subvert it from within. The Poplar Guardians, for example, were already making attempts to humanise the way in which relief was given even before the First World War. The Liberal government reacted by passing the Poor Law Relief Regulations Order of 1911, which made it illegal for relief to be given unless the claimant was put to task work, received one-half of the relief in kind, and was subjected to other stringent tests.[12] The administration of the Poor Law was, if anything, further tightened by the Liberal government.

The Liberals' response to the minority report of the Royal Commission was to establish a contributory system of relief through insurance. In the National Insurance Act of 1911, a few major industries were brought into a structure in which employers and workers paid into a fund. This fund provided the money for making payments when workers became unemployed. Although extremely limited at this time, the Act was the basis of the contributory and non-means tested structure which has co-existed with the non-contributory and means-tested framework ever since.

In Scotland, the situation of the workless was even worse. There, the parish councils were responsible under the Poor Act of 1845, but there was no absolute requirement for the councils to levy poor rates, nor to build workhouses.

Consequently, many councils had no effective machinery for relieving unemployment at all, and those out of work were thrown back on their families and charities. Although by the late nineteenth century Scottish councils were beginning to move towards English levels of expenditure on relief, they were generally still spending less by the early 1920s. The local kirk and voluntary organisations remained important sources of help for the Scottish unemployed in the inter-war years, and the struggle against charity was particularly important for the Scottish activists in the unemployed movement.[13]

These systems were only slowly modified in the inter-war years. Governments expanded the National Insurance scheme, but did so whilst trying to balance the books. In times of persistent mass unemployment, this meant that the scheme, as it gradually evolved, was always inadequate and could never amount to more than a supplement to the Poor Law system. The unemployed were invariably pushed onto the mercy of the Guardians.

Since this was the situation, large indeterminate areas remained open to bargaining. At a local level, what was the rate of relief to be? When and in what form was it to be paid? When and on what terms was task work to be done? What conditions would rule in the workhouse? These were just a few of the debatable issues.

The fact that the administration of relief was administered on a highly localised basis was very important, as it meant that the bargaining situation could be exploited even by relatively small local groupings. The workless could identify the Guardians and Relieving Officers who were meting out their treatment; rather than fighting a remote and apparently more legitimate government in far-away Westminster, they could see the opposition before them. They could see the inequalities with their own eyes; Guardians who drove around in motor cars whilst the unemployed had to walk everywhere. Their pasts were known, too, and it was often pointed out that many of those who decided the fate of the unemployed had never done any form of war service. Moreover, the remedy lay in the Guardians' hands. They could to a very large extent determine not only the rates of relief, but the whole attitude and policy of the Relieving Officers, not to mention conditions in the workhouse. On the other side, they were faced by relatively compact and cohesive working-class communities in most towns, where housing, lack of transport and poverty pushed people together. It was hardly surprising, then, that Guardians and Relieving Officers found their houses 'beset', or that Guardians found themselves opposed at elections by ratepayers sympathetic to the unemployed. The whole situation was much more conducive to collective organisation that that of the 1980s, when a highly centralised and legally regulated machine confronts a much more fragmented body of claimants.

There were a number of other important ways in which the workless were pressed together, as though governments failed to see the ways in which they themselves were encouraging solidarities to develop. Signing-on at Labour Exchanges was regular (generally twice weekly), concentrating large numbers of people together for long periods of time, and creating a Labour-Exchange subculture in which people exchanged greetings, complaints and cigarettes. The establishment of 'slave colonies' which people had to attend for weeks or months to prove their willingness to work by some Boards of Guardians even before the government equivalents were set up in the late 1920s could also reinforce solidarity. This was especially true of task work, which effectively replicated the work situation. Task work was, formally speaking, a legal requirement for out-relief, although some Guardians chose to ignore this fact. The result was often go-slows, and even strikes. The Cabinet had foreseen this problem when contemplating large-scale relief work in 1919. One of the reasons why such national work programmes were not launched was undoubtedly that they would, as a Cabinet memorandum put it, 'concentrate large masses of men violently discontented with the wages they receive'.[14] But here was a contradiction: task work might bring difficulties, but the alternative was to concede that the unemployed had a right to relief without proving their willingness to work.

The fact that the system pushed people together created a framework within which the unemployed could begin to organise themselves. But culture played an important part within that framework. In the larger towns, and in pit villages, the unemployed created their own social life. This allowed them to overcome their isolation and misery however momentarily, and to contemplate turning outwards. The result was in some areas a 'street-corner' society which was quite public. Whilst some people, like the tailors and garment workers in the East End of London, met and whiled away the time (doubtless hoping for some hint of work) in the trade union offices, pitmen stood around talking, often organising small amateur boxing bouts or football matches. In these circumstances, it was impossible to regard yourself as being the only person unemployed in the area: the human evidence stood around in public in a way which is not true today. This was a very male society. Whilst women worked intensively at home to make a little money go further, men sought the company of their mates rather than getting 'under the feet' of their wives.

Such was the background to the creation of the NUWM between the wars: large-scale structural unemployment based on the primary industries occurring within a system of relief which was recognised as inadequate yet which tended to foster solidarity. These circumstances existed in a number of countries across the world, and numerous unemployed movements were thrown up, from Haiti to New Zealand in these years. The organisations varied greatly, but they were all the products not only of the specific national context, but also of intensive activity in the most difficult circumstances. In Britain as elsewhere, highly active, politically aware and determined activists forged the unemployed movement. It was their historic achievement to create one of the world's most durable unemployed organisations in the face of the apathy and despair created by worklessness.

Notes

1 *The Third Winter of Unemployment*, Report of an Inquiry Undertaken in the Autumn of 1922, London 1922, pp.3-4; N. Branson, *Britain In the 1920s*, London 1975, p.76.
2 S. Pollard, 'The Trade Unions and the Depression of 1929-33' in H. Mommsen, D. Petzina and B. Weisbrod: (eds), *Industrielles System und politische Entwicklung in der Weimarer Republik*, Dusseldorf 1974, p.239.
3 *The Third Winter of Unemployment*, p.5.
4 A. Deacon, *In Search of the Scrounger*, London 1976, p.15.
5 H.J. Bush, 'Local, Intellectual and Policy Responses to Localised

Unemployment in the Inter-War Period', unpublished PhD thesis, Nuffield College, Oxford, 1980, p.6.

6 J.B. Jefferys, *The Story of the Engineers*, London 1945, p.198; J.E. Mortimer, *History of the Boilermakers' Society, Vol.2 1906-1939*, London 1982, p.224.

7 *The Times*, 18 February 1919.

8 A. Marwick, *Women at War, 1914-1918*, London 1977, p.73.

9 *Woman Worker*, February 1919; *Daily Herald*, 8 February 1919.

10 Ibid.

11 J. MacNicol, *The Movement for Family Allowances, 1918-45*, London 1980, pp.50-1.

12 See M.E. Rose, *The English Poor Law, 1780-1930*, London 1971.

13 See E.H. Hunt, *British Labour History, 1815-1914*, London 1981.

14 'The Unemployment Situation', Memo. September 1921. CAB 24/128. For an example of collective action among taskworkers, see *Labour's Northern Voice*, 13 August 1928.

2
A Land 'Fit For Heroes'?

From War to Peace

On 12 December 1918, a large demonstration of trade unionists, with a smattering of servicemen, took place in Newcastle. Called by 26 trade union branches and district committees, it included the young Sid Elias, then a shop steward at Palmers Jarrow yard and later chairman of the unemployed workers' movement. The demonstration was one month after the signature of the Armistice and immediately before the 'khaki' General Election in which Lloyd George triumphed with promises of a 'land fit for heroes'. A few weeks later, the Clydeside engineers were to strike for the forty-hour week in an attempt to forestall mass unemployment.

Many local engineers were already thrown out of work by the end of war production, a situation which the Coalition government had foreseen, and had made provision for by allowing them a small unemployment benefit as a 'donation'. An important principle had therefore already been conceded: that benefit could be paid quite outside of the existing schemes, and irrespective of people's contribution record. Yet this was far from enough to satisfy the demonstrators, who clearly had further expectations of what peacetime should bring. The *Newcastle Daily Journal* painted the demonstration in colourful and even heroic terms in recognition of its importance:

> With many coloured banners held aloft, thirty thousand Tyneside trade unionists took part yesterday in a march of the unemployed. They foregathered in the streets running near to the Newcastle Cattle Market, waiting solemnly for the order to

move. Some were still in their work overalls, the factory grime showing on their faces, their eyes heavy with the strain that nightshift brings.[1]

The engineers, in accordance with their position as aristocrats of labour, lined up immediately behind the workmen's band leading the march. In the middle, 'just as deeply concerned as the men' was a large body of women.[2] When the demonstrators reached Haymarket, they gathered round two platforms and cheered each new contingent of workers as they reached the meeting. A resolution was put when everyone had arrived, and certain points picked out and underlined by the trade union officials who proposed it:

> That we, the workers in the engineering and shipbuilding industries of Tyneside, view with dismay the ruthless conduct of the Government in causing thousands of our members to be discharged without having made adequate provision for their maintenance. We consider that the unemployment benefit that the Government is allowing is altogether inadequate to keep us in physical fitness in view of the present conditions; and we claim that we are fully justified in demanding that the workers should be paid their correct rate of wages during reconstruction. We also demand that the allowances of soldiers and sailors be increased so that their dependants may be enabled to live in comfort, instead of as at the present time, a state of semi-starvation. That the resolution be sent to the Prime Minister, and that he be asked to receive a deputation to fully explain the situation on Tyneside.[3]

McKenna of the Plumbers' Union stressed the importance of the resolution's demand for current wages during reconstruction, and was cheered when he said that since £6 million per day had been spent on war, the same should be spent on peace. After a similar speech by Jack Little of the Amalagamated Society of Engineers, the resolution was passed amid a storm of cheering.

This impressive demonstration, one of many held at around this time in the major industrial towns, reflected a widespread feeling among both industrial workers and servicemen that a 'land fit for heroes' was precisely what was required after the enormous sacrifices of wartime. The First World War had generated an expectation of full employment by its mobilisation of labour, and of reform through its Ministry of Reconstruction. For the first time in British industrial history, it had been demonstrated that full employment was entirely possible, and that the state was well able to play a major part in the economy without disaster resulting. Moreover, industrial workers were in confident and even aggressive mood: they saw the social and political upheavals in the defeated countries and felt inclined to question the social order in Britain.

The beginning of 1919 saw employed workers making demands on behalf of the workless, when prompted by their shop stewards. During the First World War, the shop stewards of the Amalgamated Society of Engineers had developed their organisation to the point at which they were a major force in the industry; representatives of the elite of skilled craftsmen, they had challenged the right of management unilaterally to decide matters in the workshop, and even questioned the state's right to send their members to the front. Contemptuous of the trade union officials for what they saw as capitulation to the war machine, they organised a national network. The stewards now urged their members to defend the real gains made in wartime.

In January 1919, the shop stewards at the Slough transport depot, the so-called 'soviet' led by the firebrand Tom Dingley and a young socialist toolmaker, Wal Hannington, organised a demonstration for increased benefit.[4] At the end of that month, an important battle for shorter working time broke out. The Clyde engineers struck for a forty-hour week and the restoration of their shorter wartime working periods. The strike was begun in great hope, and was led well by the shop stewards, who pulled in their union officials behind them up to and including the Scottish TUC. Yet, despite spreading to parts of England, the strike failed to acheive its main aim. It had taken place at a turning point: that moment at which unemployment was looming large enough to be an issue in the workshops, but at which workers remained strong and confident enough to resist its effects. This was the last major strike of the inter-war years behind a demand for shorter working time. Its defeat was a major blow which marked the end of the shop stewards' movement of the First World War.[5] The stewards who were sacked in large numbers after the strike for reasons of slow business and managerial revenge had little choice but to follow the exhortation of their paper *Solidarity*, and to organise outside of the workplace. According to the syndicalist theory that had tinged much of that paper's comment, they might have expected, having been deprived of their power at the point of production, to be wasting their time. But experience proved otherwise.[6]

The engineers found a ready audience among the unemployed. They had in some cases already raised the issues at work, and were therefore well placed with their own members. These members were now dispersed by the sack, but were part of a skilled elite who had long been concerned to protect themselves against unemployment, and fully grasped the importance of collective organisation. Ex-servicemen were a very different case. Few of them had been trade union members before the war, most of those who were now out of work having been too young to have worked before entering the services. Moreover, they had been subjected to much wartime propaganda denouncing trade unionists for 'stabbing the soldiers in the back'. But, like the shop stewards themselves, they put aside earlier ideas when faced with a land that was distinctly unfit for heroes. Sheer anger drove them to direct and often violent action. Above all, they wanted work and housing. Denied these basic rights, they protested vigorously. If they were to be led by shop stewards and 'agitators', then they were prepared to accept this to obtain what they wanted.

The ex-servicemen's strength of feeling could not be disregarded with impunity. These men had been involved in some of the most brutal fighting the world has ever known, and were more than willing to express themselves through violence. The mayor of Luton discovered this when he chose to celebrate the formal end of hostilities with fellow-dignitaries, but without any ex-servicemen: the Town Hall was burned down in three days of rioting and looting which brought the authorities to the point of desperation. Such powerful sentiments persisted throughout the period up to the outbreak of the Second World War. 'I was fighting for the likes of such fuckers as you in the trenches when I was fifteen, while you sat behind a desk,' one unemployed man told a Chief Relieving Officer in the late 1920s.[7] It was this sense of inequality of sacrifice and reward that allowed the ex-servicemen to overcome their wartime anti-trade union conditioning, and to follow people whom they had been told previously to regard as traitors.

During 1920, unemployment rose rapidly, and although a new national insurance scheme was introduced in November of that year, it had no immediate effect. The situation was rapidly becoming desperate for the workless. Large numbers faced eviction and starvation. Several alternatives faced people: taking what they needed from the shops, asking for charity on the streets with collecting boxes, relying on relatives for support or going to the Guardians. Many rejected the possibility of asking the Guardians for relief because of the humiliations involved: the stigma of 'being on the parish' was too great for them to accept. Starvation was becoming an imminent prospect. Labour's *Daily Herald*, edited by George Lansbury, a humane socialist with a history of concern for the unemployed and a friendship with Hannington, took a clear view of this problem. People should go to the Guardians. They had a right to live; if work could not be provided, then it was not their fault. Everyone was entitled to adequate welfare, as human beings.

The *Daily Herald*'s arguments played a crucial role in creating an atmosphere in which people were prepared to make demands. Hannington and his network of ex-shop steward and socialist comrades took the *Herald*'s logic further. Inheriting the attitudes of socialists before them, they told the workless that they should not 'starve in silence', nor should they accept 'petty doles and charities'. The new element in their propaganda was that they were arguing for a militant, national organisation. Going to the Guardians was a start, but no more. The unemployed would have to organise collectively if real improvements were to be wrested from the opposition.

The First Unemployed Committees

There was already some activity amongst the unemployed, with committees of ex-servicemen and trade unionists springing up in the towns all over Britain. But the picture was a very disparate one, with patchy coverage of the country and enormous variation in the tactics employed by each local body. Some groups were adopting self-help tactics like setting up communal kitchens, making appeals to local storekeepers for credit, collecting in the streets or sometimes protesting to the Guardians over a particular aspect of their treatment. Very often, neighbours were protecting one another from eviction. But the nearest approximation to a national network was to be found in the groups of ex-servicemen which were meeting regularly in most areas at this time. It was here that Hannington started, in a local ex-servicemen's committee in St Pancras. Before long, he was touring London, arguing for a link-up of all committees around a shared programme to form a united fighting organisation.

Hannington acknowledged that he had considerable difficulty in making his arguments out to the ex-servicemen. Many of the people attending these committees felt that it would be better to try to exploit their political advantage, and not to alienate government and Guardians alike by public protest. The young socialist engineer must have frequently wished he was back in the workshop in his first few weeks of activity. It is not hard to imagine the scepticism with which men just returned from the fire of Armageddon viewed the young idealist in their midst who had been in a reserved occupation while they were in the trenches. But it is crucial to understand that deeper feelings of class and community solidarity had survived the war, and largely overcame these sentiments, as many military intelligence files from the immediate post-war period confirm. Many ex-soldiers were more than prepared to lend Hannington an ear because of this basic sense of affinity with the young craftsman and his arguments. It is important to stress this point (recently highlighted in research) because of the way that most of the existing historical writing has uncritically followed poets and novelists in suggesting the 'separating' effect of military service.[8] In any case Hannington was very determined and persistent. Above all, he suggested, they would get nothing unless they organised together behind agreed demands. He kept pressing home the argument that they should not give in to the temptation to rely simply on local organisation putting pressure on their guardians. They should make demands on the government; but they would get nothing by simply meeting their MPs, he contended. That was simply a way of being fobbed off with sympathy. Nor should people continue to rely on charity collections, since if they were successful, government would then see an excuse for abdicating their responsibilities. This was a view of government which many ex-servicemen found overly negative. But events were soon to lend weight to Hannington's contentions.

On 18 October 1920, a demonstration was organised in support of a deputation of London mayors to the Ministry of Health to demand better treatment for the unemployed. The demonstration took place as the miners began a strike, and both the government and police were nervous. The police ferociously attacked and batoned the large crowds of unemployed. The attack was merciless and many were injured. The police had unintentionally confirmed what Hannington and his comrades had been saying about the way that ex-servicemen could expect to be rewarded for their war service.

The principal result of this battle was the formation of a London District Council of Unemployed, linking up all of the unemployed and ex-servicemen's committees in the capital by delegates meeting twice weekly. The Council (LDC) had soon organised its own small newspaper, *Out Of Work*, which helped to build an awareness of the LDC amongst the unemployed in London. The first campaign of the LDC, it was decided, was to be against the Poor Law Relief Regulation Order, which made it illegal for Guardians to give out-relief without imposing task work. With the support of the Poplar Labour Guardians, who had already defied the Order for years, and the *Daily Herald*, a series of demonstrations was launched under the slogan 'Work or Full Maintenance'. This was to be the slogan of the unemployed movement from 1920 onwards. It was a clear demand, which placed responsibility on the authorities for providing one or the other and therefore implicitly rejected the notion that the unemployed were responsible for their plight. Thousands of people participated in these first demonstrations, and caused Hannington to rejoice in what he called 'the growth of a new psychology'. This 'new psychology' was really the channelling of an existing mentality in the direction of collective action. Many of the workless already thought that they were not responsible for their position, and that they should not have to apologise for asking to be supported when they were prepared to work. The difference was that they were prepared to demonstrate and act together instead of, or in addition to, asking for people's charity.[9]

London was to be the centre of unemployed agitation in the early 1920s, and it is worthwhile looking at why this was so. Whilst it was true, as Hannington suggested, that the shop stewards were in some ways the backbone of the movement, this was not the whole story. Although stewards had been strong in some London factories, many boroughs which had been relatively untouched by either the engineering industry or the shop stewards nevertheless made a substantial contribution to the unemployed ferment. This was because of the rise of Labour politics in the capital in the preceding years. By 1920, fourteen London boroughs had Labour majorities. One of the important benefits of the rise of Labour was a number of bases for the unemployed. During the winter, when most of the unemployed agitation took place, it was essential for the unemployed to have a meeting place as a focus of organisation. Many boroughs made somewhere available. Hannington gave prominence in his account to the struggle for Islington public library, which was captured and occupied by the unemployed for their own use, until the police recaptured it. But this has to be set alongside more typical cases like that of the Finsbury Library, where the unemployed simply arranged with the Town Clerk and library committee for free use of the basement for their meetings.[10] When the unemployed of eight boroughs marched on the Islington Town Hall, having just lost the library, they were 'mopping-up' rather than beginning the attack.

Outside London, although committees were operating, they rarely had good bases. The committees were nevertheless active in many industrial centres. In Coventry, for example, almost daily demonstrations to the Guardians took place. 4,500 unemployed met and demanded that the unemployed committee and the City Council should meet the Soviet trade delegation to find out what commodities were required by the Soviets, and asked that factories should be taken over to produce them. Demonstrations were held outside factory gates to argue against overtime being worked, and to propagandise for production for need rather than profit.[11] Similar activity was being carried out in other big towns.

The committees which organised such battles, or were thrown up by them, initially attracted people from various backgrounds within the local labour and ex-servicemen's movements. Harry Young, at that time a young Communist, described them as 'a spontaneous sort of outbreak', and they certainly attracted a mixed bag.[12] The Liverpool committee, for example, included the then Communist Jack Braddock, but also embraced a syndicalist, two other Communists, a clergyman (this was quite common), an ex-Royal Navy Petty Officer, an ex-conscientious objector and a devout Catholic.[13] The clergyman was a remarkable man who was soon to play a prominent role in the Liverpool policemen's strike, the Reverend Bob Tissyman, a regular speaker at meetings of the Independent Labour Party and a strong critic of the Communist Party.[14] This committee had good links with the local Seamen's Vigilance Committee. There was also a 'number two' replacement committee which took over whilst the 'number one' committee was on trial for 'riotous assembly', and this was led by Bessie Bamber, later well-known as Bessie Braddock.[15] In Coventry, the committee had nine elected members, a minority of whom were Communists, and three co-opted members from the radical National Union of Ex-Servicemen.[16] The Cardiff body was similarly mixed, including four or five trade unionists and a few Labour Party members. They met at Friends' House and were helped by the Trades Council and the Co-op printers, who gave them free printing in return for an advertisement on the reverse side of their leaflets.[17]

The Role of Communists

The early committees invariably contained socialists who were involved in the discussions which led to the formation of the Communist Party of Great Britain (CPGB). The shop stewards were amongst these, and their organisation was one of the most important in the debates surrounding the birth of the new party. Through their political understanding, their skills as orators and writers, and above all their commitment, the early Communists put themselves at the head of the unemployed movement. It was through them that a national organisation of workless was created.

The main political component of the newly created party was the British Socialist Party, an historic champion of the unemployed. From the 1880s onwards, British socialists had argued that unemployment was a direct and inevitable result of the capitalist system. They looked forward to the time when a socialist society would ensure that nobody had to seek work in vain and everybody's potential would be utilised through useful labour. The British Socialist Party contended that the capitalist system, which failed to meet the elementary needs of so many people, and fully to utilise human resources, had to be abolished. Industry and the land had to be used for the common good and not for private profit. It was this very drive for profit which created unemployment, because it was only with such a pool of surplus labour that the wages of those in work could be kept down to the lowest possible level. Ultimately, the BSP's goal was socialism through the common ownership of the means of production, which would lead to the end of waged labour, and therefore of *un*employment.

Until the years after the First World War, unemployment was mainly approached at the propagandist level by socialists, and little attention was paid to Marx's emphasis on the need to go beyond such discussion and fuse theory and practice. The Russian Revolution changed this, and seemed to hold out the prospect of revolutionary change throughout the capitalist world. The Communist Party, soon recognised by the Third (Communist) International established by the Soviet revolutionaries as its official British section, was a small band of several thousand which was very close to the unemployed in everything except political philosophy. The majority of its members were working-class men and women immersed in the everyday realities of life in Britain's industrial cities. They knew about unemployment very much at first hand. The Communists were different to the majority of workers, however, in their confidence in, and burning commitment to, the coming British revolution. For them, the revolution was a living force and an immediate prospect. This was the vision that inspired those who attended the Unity Conference of 1920, which brought together representatives of those socialist groups which wanted to emulate the historic achievement of the Bolsheviks. The chance to 'do what they did in Russia' drew them together. The young intellectual Robin Page Arnot assured the assembled comrades that 'The Communist Party will be leading and directing the revolution when it comes,' whilst others went on to express themselves in unashamedly evangelical terms on the subject of the proposed party's historic mission.[18] Despite a fundamental difference emerging between the 'Pankhurstites' and the majority, the Communist Party of Great Britain soon began its work.

Sylvia Pankhurst and her followers grouped around the paper the *Workers' Dreadnought*, and based mainly in London's East End, were initially recognised by Lenin as the official British Section of the Third International, before it became clear to the Bolsheviks that this group was 'ultra-left'. The accusation of 'ultra-leftism' was based on the Pankhurstite refusal to seek affiliation to the Labour Party, and led to the recognition of the majority of those present at the Unity Conference, largely BSPers, as the genuine representatives of the Bolshevik tradition in Britain. The Pankhurstites were then cast into outer darkness by the CPGB, and consequently their distinctive contribution in the early days of the unemployed agitation has not been fully recognised. Many of these people, amongst whom there was a high proportion of women like Lillian Thring and Marion Phillips, had long been active among the poor of the East End. Their particular blend of socialist politics and community work gave them an intimate understanding of the problems of working-class women and the misery that unemployment brought them. Some of those involved, like Charlie Sumner of Poplar, had already been active in the pre-First World War right to work movement. But all of them shared with the CPGB an awareness of the importance of 'direct action', or organising militant protests on the ground and not placing one's hopes in elections. Indeed, few people were more passionate advocates of 'direct action' than Lillian Thring, whose distinctly 'unladylike' advice to the workless on how to remove policemen from their horses was reported with horror to the Cabinet. But as they increasingly distanced themselves from the CPGB, these people also divorced themselves, a couple of years later, from the unemployed movement. This should not cause them to be entirely forgotten, however, for they made a considerable contribution to the unemployed struggle in the early years, especially amongst women. Their experience was to be sorely missed later.

If the loss of those around the *Workers' Dreadnought* was an unfortunate one in many ways, the policy which the CPGB adopted and which brought about the split was very appropriate for building an unemployed movement. Until the late 1920s, the Communist Party and the unemployed movement benefited greatly from being part of what was by today's standards a very unsectarian left. This was largely because of the CPGB's policy of the 'United Front', which came in at the end of 1921. The strategy came from the Communist International and required Communist Parties to approach leaders of reformist bodies such as the Labour Party with requests for them to unite in action to acheive specific limited aims. The reformists, so the theory went, would either be 'exposed' by their refusal, or the effectiveness of Communist politics would be shown in the ensuing struggle. The United Front policy dovetailed neatly with the requirements of building an unemployed movement, for whom external relations with other labour movement bodies were of tremendous importance. It allowed the unemployed movement to capitalise on sympathy within the Labour Party and trade unions for their cause.

Wal Hannington, the young Communist and agitator of the London District Council of the Unemployed, was quick to grasp the importance of the United Front policy, and forged good links with George Lansbury and the *Daily Herald* in the early period of agitation. In view of the significant position Hannington already occupied among the unemployed, it is worth looking more closely at him as an individual.

Wal Hannington remains a peculiarly anonymous figure, despite his many books including *Never On Our Knees*, an autobiography which reveals little of his personality. Born in 1896, the son of a bricklayer and hardworking mother, he was one of seven children brought up in a three-storied house in Camden Town. After a number of jobs, he was apprenticed as a toolmaker, and joined the elite Amalgamated Society of Toolmakers in 1915. He thereby became a member of the upper echelons of the labour aristocracy within engineering; the toolmakers were a tiny craft society who jealously guarded their privileges and position within the industry. That same year, he also joined the British Socialist Party. Les Moss worked with him at the Beta Engineering Company in Kentish Town, where Hannington was his foreman. Moss recalls him as

> The most peculiar foreman I've ever had in my life. He didn't care about the firm, he only cared about the workers there ... Walter was a bloke who used to cheat the management and assist us if we didn't do much work. He used to say, 'Well, you can't do any more, can you?' He also liked us and we got on very well. The thing about Walter Hannington was that he was a great propagandist, as you may know if you've read any of his books. He'd sit us down and preach Marxism to us nearly through the night, and it's true we hardly did any work sometimes.[19]

Hannington took Moss to his BSP branch. This was no ordinary branch, having been adopted as the political home of a group of exiled Russians which included Litvinov, Chicherin and Petrov.[20] It is little wonder, then, that when the Russian Revolution came, Hannington took care to impress its historical significance on Moss. Many years later, he recalled the dramatic personal effect it had on him: 'Instantly, I became alert, I became vitally aroused and excited ... a surge of enthusiasm arose within me ...'[21] If his own account is to be believed, the Russian upheaval marked a political turning point of massive significance which affected him emotionally as well as politically. From the moment of the CPGB's foundation, Hannington was a party man. It was where he found himself and his friends.

Hannington already had many of the qualities which he brought to the unemployed movement, and used them to effect on the London District Council. The first of these was great physical strength. A well-built man, he boxed (to his wife Winnie's occasional annoyance), swam daily, irrespective of the weather, and rejoiced in long walks.[22] Apart from one short spell of illness in the 1920s, his health was to hold despite imprisonment, Hunger Marches and privation until well beyond the end of the Second World War. Another was a meticulous approach to everything that he did. A working class autodidact of the type described by Stuart Macintyre and Jonathan Rée, he studied and wrote whenever he had a spare moment. The result of this was a stream of articles in the socialist and unemployed press of great clarity and insight, which may well deserve publication today as documents of lasting significance. We are not used to thinking of Hannington as a theoretician, but he was a clear thinker, an able writer and above all a good strategic general. Lastly, he was already an excellent speaker. T.A. Jackson felt that he needed 'no testimonials' from those who had heard him, whilst Walton Newbold compared his oratorical gifts to those of that earlier champion of the unemployed, Victor Grayson.[23]

Hannington was already working extremely hard to make the London District Council into an effective campaigning force. By travelling round from committee to committee, getting them to fall in behind a common policy, he was not only forging them into a unit, but was simultaneously laying the foundations of what he realised would have to be a national organisation. In this work, membership of the CPGB was a crucial asset. Although the Communist Party was as yet a tiny organisation, it began to develop a national network of paid organisers, and a press, which provided an essential parallel structure to complement and support that of the unemployed. An organisation of workless in isolation may well have been too impoverished and unstable to survive. But the CPGB, like the unemployed committees, did not yet have a developed national structure. Nor did it have a fractional machine bringing together Communists in the unemployed movement until 1924 at the earliest.[24] But as they grew, consolidated and 'Bolshevised', the Communists gave life to the National Unemployed Workers' Committee Movement.

Notes

1 *Newcastle Daily Journal*, 13 December 1918.
2 Ibid.
3 Ibid.
4 *Workers' Dreadnought*, 11 January 1919.
5 I.MacLean, *The Legend of Red Clydeside*, Edinburgh 1983, p.115; M.Lomax; 'The Forty Hours Strike, Glasgow 1919', unpublished MA Dissertation, University of Warwick, 1974, pp.127-32.
6 *Solidarity* (West London edition), 4 February 1921. See also the interview with Hannington in *The Times*, 4 January 1923, in which he is reported as regarding the organised unemployed movement as simply the

continuation in a different situation of the shop stewards' movement of the First World War.

7 E. Benson, *To Struggle Is to Live*, vol.2:*Starve Or Rebel, 1927-71*, Newcastle 1980, pp.52-3.

8 See A. Englander, 'Soldiers and Socialism: the National Union of Ex-Servicemen and the British Labour Movement' in R. Samuel (ed.), *The Making of British National Identity*, London 1987.

9 W. Hannington, *Unemployed Struggles*, London 1936 (reprinted 1979), pp.17-8.

10 *The Times*, 26 November 1920. See J. Bush, *Behind The Lines*, London 1984, Chapter 7, for the growth of the Labour Party in London during the First World War.

11 *The Times*, 5 and 6 October 1920.

12 Interview with Harry Young, 23 September 1983.

13 M.Toole, *Mrs Bessie Braddock, MP* London 1957, p.61.

14 Manuscript biography of Bob Tissyman, kindly lent me by the author, Alan O'Toole.

15 Ibid.

16 F.W.Carr, 'Engineering Workers and the Rise of Labour in Coventry, 1914-1939', unpublished PhD Thesis, University of Warwick, 1978, pp.117-8.

17 Interview with Sid Elias, 25 June 1983.

18 Sylvia Pankhurst's notes on CPGB meeting, n.d., (International Library of Social History, Amsterdam)

19 L. Moss, *Live And Learn*, Brighton 1979, pp.20-1.

20 T.H.E. Young, 'Investigation Into the Origin and Development of the Communist Party In Islington' (essay kindly lent me by the author), p.8.

21 W. Hannington, *Never On Our Knees*, London 1967, p.49.

22 Interview with Winnie Hannington by Doug Low (date unknown).

23 T. Jackson, unpaginated draft of *Solo Trumpet*, Part 2 (Marx Memorial Library); J.T.W. Newbold, unpaginated manuscript autobiography (John Rylands University Library, Manchester).

24 R. Palme Dutt, Diary, 2 October 1923 (CPGB Library).

3

Towards a National Unemployed Movement, 1921-23

As everyone involved appreciated only too well, the problems of the unemployed were national in scope, and could therefore only be adequately dealt with by government. The first task which the London District Council set itself was accordingly the creation of a truly national movement of the unemployed which would draw in all militant groupings. On New Year's Day 1921, the LDC stated this aim in the *Communist*, and reaffirmed its determination to reach its goal in the first edition of its own lively newspaper *Out Of Work*, which appeared soon afterwards. The *Communist* published a circular issued by the LDC to all Trades Council secretaries and Labour Parties. It claimed that the LDC already represented 250,000 unemployed in London, but declared that a national body allied to the labour movement was needed to bring pressure 'to settle once and for all the unemployed problem'. The tone of the circular was typically direct and uncompromising: in the past, the workless had 'tolerated petty doles and charity, but now our Council is determined that the government must make very different decisions'. The LDC's aims were given as work or full maintenance at trade union rates of pay, and the re-establishment of trade with Russia. The second of the two demands was seen as being of equal importance to the first: if instead of spending huge sums on fighting the Russian Revolution, the government expanded trade with the Soviet Union, then work could be provided for many, and full maintenance paid to the rest.[1] This was a key argument because it answered the question of how these demands could be met, whilst at the same time drawing on the extensive sympathy which existed among working people for the new Soviet government. The circular demanded the support of the whole working-class movement on the grounds that unemployment affected everyone by undermining the bargaining power of those in work. Circularised bodies were asked either to put the LDC in touch with the secretary of any unemployed committee, or, if one did not exist, to call a public meeting to set one up. Industrial action would be needed, and recipients of the circular were asked to pass a resolution to the National Council of Action (a joint organisation of trade union and labour representatives) calling on it to organise a National Convention at which the unemployed could be represented, and stating that if the demands were not met, then there would be a 'down tools' policy. The letter ended by appealing for donations to build a national organisation of unemployed, stressing that every one of the LDC's members was an active trade unionist. Since Lloyd George had broken his promise, the unemployed were 'morally justified' in using any and every means to get justice. The circular was signed by Holt (an engineer), Jennett (an ex-serviceman) and Phillips for the LDC.[2]

The demands which the LDC had made on organised labour were an important feature of their appeal, but the traditions of the shop stewards' movement and the revolutionary theory of the CPGB meant that they actually held out little hope for real support from labour leaders. When the Labour Party held a national conference on unemployment at the end of February 1921, the *Communist* doubted that anything positive would be achieved. The conference was to report back on the feelings of Labour Party and trade union members about taking 'direct action' on unemployment. Yet the meeting place was kept secret, and a motion passed against hearing from the unemployed themselves. Strike action was rejected, and people were simply advised to join the Labour Party. Jimmy Thomas, the right-wing leader of the railwaymen, was in the chair and refused to allow any motion other than an officially prepared one to be put. The meeting ended in uproar caused by delegates incensed by Thomas's ruling, and was followed by a march of 10,000 workless from outside the congress hall (the venue had not been a very well-kept secret) to Hyde Park.[3] Years later,

Hannington was to criticise the labour leaders in general terms for this display. But his reaction at the time was far more scathing. The hopes of 'the great army of workers' had been frustrated by the 'Yellow Trade Unionists'. The conference had left the problem 'precisely as before'. He continued:

> *I definitely accuse the Labour leaders of cowardice. What have they done since the Conference of January 27th to test the feelings of their members on turning their resolutions into acts? They have refused to carry out their own resolutions.*
>
> (Italics in original, R.C.)[4]

The Labour Party's demand for forty shillings a week for an unemployed married man was 'an insult to the unemployed' as it was worth only seventeen shillings in pre-war terms. Appealing to the workless to 'go down fighting', he called on them to read the Communist Party's literature.[5] In another piece, he called the conference 'Not only an absolute farce, but an abdication'.[6] Hannington's attitude to the Labour leaders, although later diluted, could not have been sharper. But the emphasis could now be put on building an independent organisation which would co-operate with labour movement bodies, but would also refuse to subordinate its own interests to those of their 'yellow' leaders.

On 15 April 1921, delegates from unemployed committees met at the International Socialist Club in London to discuss the formation of a national unemployed movement. It was 'Black Friday', which, as G.D.H. Cole wrote, 'brought an epoch in the labour movement's history to an end'.[7] On that day, the leaders of the railwaymen and transport workers instructed their members not to strike in support of the miners. The supposedly unbeatable Triple Alliance of the three unions had collapsed ignominiously. Even as the unemployed movement was being established, then, the trade union leaders were demonstrating that they had no real support to offer fellow trade unionists in, let alone out of, work.

Attendance at the meeting was disappointingly low, as many committees were prevented from sending delegates by shortage of funds. There were just 81 representatives of 50 committees present. Since it was claimed that the LDC already had 30 committees affiliated, it seems likely that at least half of the delegates were from London.[8] The labour press largely overlooked the gathering and the usually sympathetic *Daily Herald* also neglected it. Even the generally over-zealous police spies did not report to the Cabinet until mid-September.[9]

The police report of the first national meeting is the fullest that we have, as the Special Branch were very active in reporting on 'revolutionary organisations' at this time. The report stated that the aims of the new movement were: the removal of the capitalist system; work or full maintenance on trade union rates; a trading agreement with Russia and recognition of the Soviet government. The meeting elected a National Administrative Council (NAC) thus directly adopting the title of the shop stewards' equivalent body consisting of a chairman (Jack Holt), a secretary (Percy Haye), both of whom had been active in the shop stewards' NAC, five delegates from areas of England and a women's representative. The report described all those elected as 'Communists', and although this is true as far as we know, the writer wrote in such a way as to suggest that he thought that anyone attending such a meeting was by definition a 'Communist'. The report took some pains to link the new organisation to the Communist Party: its headquarters were at the International Socialist Club, described as being wholly under the control of the CPGB, whilst the unemployed organisation was affiliated to the International Union of the Unemployed.[10] Recent violent disturbances among the unemployed in ports such as Liverpool, Dundee, Bristol and Sunderland were ascribed to the apparently enormous influence of Anton Beratz, the Communist International's representative in Britain, who had recently issued instructions to concentrate on sea ports.[11] The meeting was, it appeared, dominated by Communists, as the policies adopted showed, but, as we have seen, the organisation was at a local level, far from being a Communist 'front' in the sense that it was one in which party members alone were active. In any case, the 'movement' did not exist as such at this point: it remained little more than an abstraction until the first national activities were successfully carried through. After the first national meeting the National Unemployed Workers' Committee

Movement was announced as having been formed, but it remained nothing more than a hopeful umbrella term for a loose federation of local committees. In fact, this remained a problem for the putative movement for years to come.

The March to the Labour Party Conference

The first activity carried out on behalf of the movement nationally was as London-based as the national meeting. It was decided to march from London to the Labour Party Conference in Brighton in the summer of 1921. The aim of the march was to present the arguments and demands of the new movement to the delegates. Hannington had not set the rank and file too difficult a task. Many of the volunteers were ex-servicemen, and long marches were familiar to them; in this case the distance was relatively short and the weather reasonable. It was a useful rehearsal for the Hunger March to come.

The operation was executed in something of a military fashion. When they came into Brighton, they were met by a contingent of local unemployed, who marched past and 'fell in at the rear'. Hannington went on:

> The way they marched into Brighton was magnificent; every man was in step. Hundreds of people lined the route to see our arrival. The one thing they marvelled at was the well-drilled and disciplined way in which the men marched after doing seventeen miles that day. Many people passed comments on the smartness displayed.[12]

The deputation which addressed the Conference presented the NUWCM's demands and bitterly attacked the leaders of the TUC and Labour Party for their inactivity. This helped to alienate still further the leadership of the Labour Party, but the march was not therefore a complete failure. Many of the delegates became aware of the unemployed movement for the first time and support from Labour Party activists was often important in the establishment of local committees. The unemployed movement had announced its arrival as the Labour Party's conscience in welfare matters. Moreover, the march itself had been an important experience for those who went on it: it allowed the unemployed to assert their dignity against the images of degeneracy and criminality that were projected onto them. The idea of such marches was not new: before the First World War, contingents of workless from the right to work agitation had tramped to London. But the emphasis on discipline was new, and honed an existing weapon to a sharp edge.

Unemployment rose to 18 per cent in the summer of 1921, and benefit was reduced. Practically every industrial area was in a ferment as large numbers of unemployed protested by demonstrating, squatting in unoccupied houses, looting shops, picketing guardians' houses, rioting and holding meeting after meeting outside Labour Exchanges. Unemployed revolt was reaching a crescendo. Unemployed committees tried to give some form to this inchoate protest. An example of the sort of action which committees were organising was the occupation of the Wandsworth Workhouse. The local unemployed had been told that they would no longer be given out-relief and would have to apply instead to the workhouse for entry. Their response was to do so in a co-ordinated way, so as to swamp the institution with people. At six o'clock the next morning, one thousand people, including many women and children, formed up in a column and set off for the workhouse. The women and children were drawn up on the outside of the column, so that if the police attacked it would, in the words of the committee, be a 'delicate job'. At the workhouse, 700 unemployed entered as previously agreed, and once inside, they took over by sheer force of numbers. They refused to recognise the authority of the Poor Law officers, and conducted a determined battle for better treatment and conditions than those they were living with were receiving. One man, for example, refused to give his child the bread provided, throwing it across the room and shouting that this was what they were offered in return for fighting for their country. The demands of the occupiers were relayed through the elected unemployed committee, while a red flag was hoisted on to the roof as the song was sung below. Eventually, the Guardians agreed to extend out-relief.[13]

In order to try to co-ordinate the various local actions and campaigns that were already going on, the NAC declared the week ending Saturday 15 October a national week of action. The week was to climax on the Thursday, when a 'Monster

Demonstration' was called for each area. The NAC wrote to each committee in unequivocal terms: 'On this day, all unemployed committees throughout the country must demonstrate their masses in full force. This must be one the like of which Britain has never seen.'[14] Here was the first test of the amount of support which the NAC could generate. It is hard to be precise about how many people participated in the week of action, but police reports would tend to support an estimate of several hundred thousands in the different provincial centres alone. In London, the leaders of the unemployed movement met the Minister of Health, there was an upward revision of scales and, for the first time, the principle of payment for dependants was conceded. The mobilisation, then, had been huge, and it had brought results. The concessions were vital to the new movement: they had shown that mass action by the unemployed could bring results, and that they were not powerless because they were out of work. The movement's paper *Out Of Work* triumphantly reported that the deputation had been seen by the Ministers because the ministers admitted that 'THEY REPRESENTED A LARGE BODY OF ORGANISED PEOPLE (Quite correct: we do).[15] The National Unemployed Workers' Committee Movement had come through its first major test with flying colours. Mass mobilisation and results had been achieved very rapidly, because the mood of the unemployed was right and the new movement's leadership had realised this and struck while the iron was hot.

All over the country, the unemployed committees had approached their local Guardians with the demands of the movement. It many areas, this meant that the Guardians were for the first time faced with a challenge to their assumed and long-standing right to dispense relief to the unemployed as they saw fit. The whole nature and tenor of the discussions is therefore intrinsically interesting as a study in social relations at this particular point. There is a record of one of these discussions which occurred when a deputation visited the Cardiff Guardians on Saturday 15th with a demonstration of several thousands behind them.

The chairman of the Guardians was Archdeacon Buckley, who tried to defuse the situation by opening in a conciliatory manner. The Board, he pointed out, was no longer a body of

'Mr Bumbles', but had on it many people 'activated by Christian motives'. He would not, he said, be a Guardian if he had no 'sympathetic ideas', and thought it right that all cases should be treated 'in the spirit of sympathy and of helping our fellow men'. But the Archdeacon also felt he had to point out that unemployment was an international problem and not solely a British one. The sting came at the end of his speech, when he insisted that the ratepayers of Monmouthshire were already overburdened. Here was the old argument that earned the Guardians the title of 'Guardians of the Rates'. Potter, replying for the unemployed committee, began by saying that they 'were not there because we wanted to be'. They were out for work, not doles. Most of them were 'self-respecting citizens, and were out for the peace of Cardiff; it was the Guardians duty to co-operate with them'. The unemployed were not trying to increase the national burden, but it was the duty of the nation to organise for peace as it had done for war. He pointed out that Lloyd George had shaken hands with Sinn Feiners, but refused to do so with the unemployed. 'The unemployed knew there was a solution to unemployment, but not under capitalism,' he said, and the threat of a new social order was accompanied by a more direct threat when he said that they were reasonable men, but others were having to be restrained from violence. Moreover, there was a threat to public morality as women could be forced 'onto the streets'. Another member of the committee opened by saying that they would get satisfaction if they had to stay there until 1924. Challenging any one of the Guardians to live on relief, he asserted that boys would not be able to fight for their country when they grew up, if they grew up on such a diet. Sid Elias, secretary of the committee, picked up on the Archdeacon's opening remark about sympathy:

> It was not sympathy they wanted, it would not fill empty bellies. Some of these men had almost got out of control, and were asking that something be done for them. Today, some of them had been lying out in dust carts. In 1914, the slogan was that a grateful country would never forget them.

After further statements, the deputation withdrew while the Guardians considered the case that had been put to them. The Guardians later called in the committee and announced numerous improvements in the scales, and the way they were administered. It is interesting to read in the record that this did not satisfy the deputation. They felt that the unemployed were still not being recognised as full citizens with equal rights, and said that the consequence might well be violence. A Labour Guardian characterised this as 'wild talk'. He goaded the committee by accusing them of not being able to control their followers. Price replied that he did not control them, but they controlled him.[16] In this case as in many others, it was already clear that some Labour Guardians were not the allies that the unemployed felt they should be, and saw their loyalty as lying with their fellow Guardians rather than with the workless.

The Cardiff Guardians had been challenged by the deputation's assertion that the unemployed were respectable members of the nation who were entitled to better treatment than vagrants, and intended to get it. There was always behind their remarks, as the Guardians noted on several occasions, a more or less open threat of violence. The combination of the two brought results. But what was remarkable was that the threats were being made at all.

Such a discussion would have been unimaginable seven or eight years previously; Guardians had not heard such language since the mid-nineteenth century. What was more, they felt compelled to respond. The old Poor Law system and the entire paternalistic philosophy which underlay it was being challenged in radical fashion and on a national scale.

Building the Movement

In the seventeenth edition of *Out Of Work*, Hannington announced that the unemployed movement was 'Getting Them On The Run'. Significant concessions were being won up and down the country as a result of the national week of action. The unemployed agitation was at a peak, and *Out Of Work* increased its sales as it was launched as a national NUWCM newspaper.

The movement was now being built apace in the localities. Advice was being dispensed by the NAC on how to organise locally on a daily and sometimes hourly basis. Committees were being set up all over Britain, and voluntary organisers were beginning to be appointed. The precise mechanics of setting up a committee were discussed by Percy Kealey, a leading ex-shop steward recently elected Northern Area Organiser, in a letter to an activist in mid-1921:

> The first essential move towards establishing an Unemployed Movement is a Mass meeting of the people concerned, the position of the unemployed [sic], and the necessity of a co-ordinated movement to deal with the problem, putting clearly before the meeting and arising therefrom a committee elected.
>
> Upon election the first duty of the committee should be to immediately approach the Guardians of the Poor by DEMONSTRATION and demand adequate maintenance; this should if possible be done peacably and the demands substantiated by local information re the cost of keeping the inmates of the workhouse etc. etc.
>
> My experience teaches me that a Committee of twelve *active Class Conscious Comrades* is sufficient to meet the needs of a local movement divided, of course, into its sub-committees for detailed matters such as Board of Guardians, Labour Exchange, General Purposes, etc. (Emphases in original, R.C.) [17]

Kealey's advice was that of the experienced labour movement cadre, and he was of course outlining a model arrangement. But many committees, while falling short of such counsel, sprang up and organised themselves more or less effectively. Before long, area conferences were held to co-ordinate these bodies.

The Northern Area Conference heard from Wakefield of the NAC that 70 committees would soon be functioning in the Northern Area. Many delegates reported on their work locally. The Sheffield committee was a particularly lively one: each week, four classes were held on industrial history and economics, and 100 children attended the NUWCM Sunday School, 'there to be educated as to their class position'. This was in addition to their agitational and advice work. The Conference, prompted by Percy Haye the National Secretary, adopted a set of financial proposals put to all Area Conferences. Under these arrangements, each committee was to forward a quarter of its income to the District Council. 10 per cent of branch receipts would be sent on to the NAC, and

the rest retained by the District. The arrangements were
designed to allow committees to keep most of their income,
whilst supporting a national headquarters. They were at this
point favourable to the committees when compared both to
some trade unions and to their own position a decade later.
The Amalgamated Engineering Union (in which most of the
NUWCM leadership was involved) allowed its branches less
financial autonomy than the unemployed movement. In time,
local committees found their financial room for manoeuvre
moving in a similar direction, with an increasing number of
national levies being imposed on them.[18]

On 26-7 November 1921 the NUWCM held its first full
national Conference in Manchester against a background of
steady increases in membership all over the country. The
Conference attracted 150 delegates, and the debates were
lively to the point of riotousness. In his report on the meeting,
Hannington remarked on the persistent outbreaks of uproar
and confusion in response to some speakers, which Jack Holt,
in the chair, had continually to struggle to bring under
control. Hannington, although he was later to write a book on
meeting procedure, was inclined to look with indulgence upon
this, and interpret it as a sign of enthusiasm although there
were others from the controlled and sedate traditions of skilled
unionism who thought it deplorable. Hannington felt that it
was precisely such enthusiasm which had pulled several new
committees into the Conference and the movement.

The most important body of unemployed committees to
have kept aloof from the NUWCM were those in Scotland.
Many of the Scottish activists had been strongly influenced by
the Marxist propagandist John MacLean and his group of
mendicant socialist speakers, the Tramp Trust. MacLean,
who was very well respected among Scottish radicals, had
refused to join the Communist Party mainly because he
believed that there was a need for, and a possibility of, a
separate Scottish Communist Party. He was particularly
active, together with his close comrades such as Harry
McShane, amongst the unemployed, and was scornful of the
NUWCM, which he criticised as nothing more than a network
of committees. MacLean and McShane had held off the
CPGB on the Glasgow Unemployed Committee, but the
November 1921 Conference, Hannington noted with pleasure,

was the first to attract a substantial Scottish delegation.[19] The other Scottish committees were already moving towards the unemployed movement. In July 1922, McShane broke with his mentor to join the CPGB, and soon became Hannington's Scottish right-hand man.[20] Scotland was already a strong area for unemployed organisations, and their move into the new body gave it a much better claim to being a genuinely British or, for some, an International Unemployed Workers' Committee Movement.

The Manchester Conference took a number of important organisational decisions. The NUWCM was divided into seven divisions with one unpaid organiser in each. There was to be an unpaid national women's organiser, and Lillian Thring, the editor of *Out Of Work*, was elected to this position. There was also to be a paid national organiser's job, to which Hannington was elected. Wherever possible, groups of committees in an area were to elect a district committee for co-ordination and direction. In addition, the Conference clarified the NUWCM's policies on relations with employed workers. It was stressed that one of the organisation's main objectives was to build bridges between the unemployed and the employed. The leaders of the NUWCM saw the fate of the workless as being inextricably linked with that of those in work. The NUWCM, as far as they were concerned, was an integral part of the labour movement. Indeed, it was essential in their opinion that the NUWCM was fully recognised as such. The Conference therefore decided to seek affiliation to the TUC. Members of the NUWCM were also urged to give active support to workers in dispute, an injunction that was considered so important that it was put on the tiny membership cards.[21] They were also urged to raid and picket factories where regular overtime was being worked, or wage cuts accepted without a fight.

The Factory Raids

The 'factory raid' tactic had been used on several occasions before the Conference, but was popularised there. The London unemployed had already insinuated themselves into factories where overtime was being worked, and argued with those inside that they were doing them out of employment. So that this should not be seen simply as a demand being made on the workforce by the unemployed, attempts were also made to negotiate on pay and conditions, especially where these fell below the 'district rate' stipulated as a minimum by the AEU. This was an important part of the raids; their object was to drive home the message that the employed and unemployed had a real common interest.

Hannington ascribed great importance to the factory raids, comparing their relevance to the *Daily Herald*'s call to 'Go to the Guardians'. In an early edition of *Out Of Work*, he wrote: 'George Lansbury's advice was: "March to the Guardians". My advice is: "March to the Factories".'[22] Hannington's personal commitment, combined with the strength of the movement in London and the relatively buoyant local labour market, helped to create the conditions which made the raids possible there. Elsewhere, the tactic does not seem to have been adopted on any great scale.

Between the Manchester Conference and the beginning of 1922, the London unemployed committees carried out some fifteen raids on factories where large amounts of overtime were being worked. Probably the largest raid took place at the Ediswan Electric Lamp Company at Ponders End, London, led by Hannington and Lillian Thring. 300 unemployed rushed the main gates at 4.15 p.m., and in a carefully prepared and efficiently executed operation gained entry to a workshop in which electric light bulbs were stored. The engineers among the unemployed soon switched off the machinery. Trouble with the police was rendered unlikely inside the factory because of the large store of bulbs. A meeting was held in the workshop, in which Lillian Thring explained to the large number of women she attracted why overtime was a problem both for them and for the unemployed, whilst Hannington negotiated in an office with a director, Dr Hyatt, who had appeared on the scene. Hannington extracted an agreement from Hyatt that all overtime would cease at Christmas, and that if overtime should be deemed necessary in the future, then the company would first try to find sufficient extra workers from the Labour Exchange, local union branches and the unemployed committee. Hannington's powers of persuasion were such that he managed to get Hyatt to make these promises in front of the workers' meeting, and, what was more, to get him to promise publicly that he would try to get them paid for the time lost through no fault of their own, when the next directors meeting took place. 200 police soon arrived, but there was no violence, and the raiders left in a column, singing 'The Red Flag' and 'The Internationale' to be greeted by a huge crowd which had gathered outside of the works.[23]

Another account of a factory raid, this time on the AEC factory, also in North London, was given by Hannington himself to Len Choulerton, later the AEU convenor at that factory. Once again, it illustrates Hannington's acute tactical sense:

> Wally told me a story when they invaded the AEC factory, went in and, of course, they were working a lot of overtime which is happening now and nobody's saying a word about it, overtime's increased in this very period when we've got all these unemployed. Anyway, they went in there ... they went in this plant ... they took off their coats, the company didn't supply you with uniform then, with overalls, so Wally just says, 'Take off your coats and stand alongside the others,' and of course when the police came they were saying, 'Well, he's a raider, and he's a raider.' And when they came out, and I don't think this is in his book, when they came out, the police were waiting for them and they had to go down the drive in the AEC, they drew their truncheons, and Wally saw this heap of old metal and bearings and things and he said 'Make for the scrap heap,' and they all picked up the lumps and they were all ready, and Wally bravely went down to the Inspector and said, 'Now look, unless you call your men off, you see what our fellers are loaded with, now there's going to be a bloody battle and some heads are going to go in, you've either got to call them men off, you know we've done what we wanted to do, the press knows it, everybody knows it, we've finished, we're going.' Anyhow, after a bit of an argument, the copper called his men off, and Wally, I don't think this is in his book either, when they got outside, he said, 'Len, we had all this scrap metal, we made a few bob out of it!'[24]

The negotiating skills, courage and ability to turn a difficult situation to advantage were typical of Hannington, and it is understandable that people were generally reluctant to undertake raids without him.

Hannington pointed out in *Unemployed Struggles* that the

factory raids had reduced overtime in some cases, improved rates of pay and conditions in others and raised the overtime issue in the AEU itself.[25] Momentarily, some sort of unity between the employed and unemployed was being acheived. But this much hoped for unity was only short-lived, as the demands raised by the AEU for less overtime led directly to the employers locking out the engineers and inflicting a severe defeat upon them. After the lock-out, there was no recurrence of the factory raid tactic because those vestiges of confidence which had remained among engineering workers and which had allowed them to lend an ear to their unemployed mates were destroyed.

The 1922 Engineering Lock-out

During the spring and early summer of 1922, the NUWCM played a major role in supporting the AEU through the national engineering lock-out initiated by the employers to enforce 'the right to manage', systematic overtime and pay reductions. Those engineers who accepted the employers' terms were invited to work, and picketing, much of which was done by the unemployed, was therefore necessary. Hannington had called on the AEU to make a stand, and he told the union that it had nothing to fear from the unemployed, but could rely on their assistance: 'Let the AEU give the lead, AND THEY WILL FIND THE ORGANISED UNEMPLOYED STANDING SHOULDER TO SHOULDER WITH THEM, ready to picket the jobs, aye, even ready to raid the factory if blacklegs are employed.'[26] The following edition of *Out Of Work* carried a notice boxed in the centre of its front page reminding all committees of the NUWCM's third rule, which stated that the unemployed committees were pledged to assist workers who were on strike or in dispute.[27] Many NUWCM members also held AEU cards, and in several areas they played a leading part in the dispute. In Birkenhead, a member of the movement was chair of the lock-out committee whilst another was in charge of the picketing squads. In several districts, including Edinburgh, Renfrew, Coventry and Luton, NUWCM members were co-opted onto lock-out committees. In Manchester, the unemployed movement's headquarters were put at the lock-out committee's ,disposal. The unemployed committees supplied hundreds of pickets; indeed, in some districts they seem to have been the only pickets available.[28]

By the middle of June, the AEU had capitulated. About 250,000 workers had suffered a humiliating defeat after a long dispute, and now had to work under much worse terms. Many were to leave the union. It may be, as L.J. Macfarlane noted, that the Communist Party could 'congratulate itself' on the part it had played, but the fact remained that this was a crushing defeat for the labour movement as a whole.[29] There were short-term gains for the NUWCM: some branches, like Deptford, increased their membership, whilst others, like Aylesbury, improved their finances with help from the AEU.[30] Also, the NUWCM had begun to establish a reputation for supporting trade unionists in dispute that helped them maintain good trade union links; their proud claim that the NUWCM was 'blackleg-proof' had been amply justified. But the defeat of the lock-out meant that there was less and less opportunity for them to show their solidarity. Whilst in 1921 the number of working days lost through strikes stood at over 85,000,000, it was 8,000,000 by 1925 and only just over 1,000,000 in 1927 and 1928.[31] Opportunities for 'slipstreaming' the activity of employed workers and thereby overcoming the isolation of the workless became increasingly restricted in the next few years.

The end of the engineering lock-out contributed to the movement's financial difficulties because it meant the end of small amounts of assistance from the AEU in many localities. There were perpetual financial problems in the unemployed movement, but here was the first crisis. Head office had to publish a desperate appeal in *Out Of Work*, saying that it was in danger of closing down and asking for contributions to a Special Emergency Fund.[32] Unstable membership, poor income from subscriptions and a 'summer slump' in activity had conspired to create this crisis. A new and more efficient system for collecting subscriptions had been devised, but had not yet been fully implemented by the committees.[33] What was needed was a new upsurge of enthusiasm and activity to replenish the paying membership and the NUWCM's coffers.

The government itself provided a stimulus to recruitment in the form of 'the gap'. This was a period of six weeks during which the long-term unemployed were suspended from benefit. Brought in just before the end of the engineering dispute, it was called 'a challenge thrown' by Hannington. A week of agitation was conducted in June, and after six weeks of agitation, made more effective because the local authorities were also pressurising the government since they were having to relieve the victims, the government largely gave in. 'The gap' was reduced from six weeks to one.[34]

The First National Hunger March, 1922-23

Buoyed up by success in fighting the 'gap', the unemployed movement reached a climax to their early period of success with a genuinely national Hunger March. The Brighton march had been a London-based affair with the aim of putting its case to the Labour Party Conference; the Hunger March was a nationally organised event to pressurise the government. It was an altogether more ambitious and more successful undertaking.

The idea for the march does not appear to have come from the national leadership of the NUWCM. The Birmingham committee decided to send thirty unemployed on a march to London to publicise the movement's demands, possibly in response to a leader in the *Daily Herald* which had said that it would be a good idea for groups to march from all over the country to see the relevant Ministers. The left-wing intellectual J.T.Walton Newbold, who had been a close associate of the unemployed movement since its inception, picked up this idea and touched on it in an article on the work of the Barrow committee in *Out Of Work*.[35] The national leadership soon responded to the ideas being mooted, and by 16 September Holt and Haye had circularised all committees, asking them to send contingents: 'The bigger the contingent the better but DON'T BRING OR SEND OTHER THAN THOSE WHO CAN BE RELIED UPON.'[36]

During mid-November, numerous groups of marchers arrived in London. They had all resisted being treated as 'casuals' or vagrants in the parishes they had visited on the way, and were put up in Poplar when they arrived in the capital. Groups of marchers continued to arrive right up until the end of the year. The number present in London varied,

but at its height was probably around 2,000. The mar‹
conducted a tremendous agitation during their stay. ‹
began with a mass demonstration on 23 November, wʰen
Parliament opened, in which some 50,000 people participated.
The whole of the winter was taken up with a constant
succession of meetings in and around London, as the
marchers did not return home until asked to do so by their
leaders on 20 February. During this time, attempts were made
to broaden the ferment beyond London, with two 'recruiting
marches' making expeditions out of the capital to try to bring
some unemployed into the agitation and the movement, and
the TUC agreeing to a national demonstration on 7 January.
The support gained by the movement pushed Ministers into
receiving a deputation, and at this meeting the Birmingham
delegation was astute enough to gain maximum publicity by
ensuring that the *Daily Herald* reporter was asked in.[37] As a
result, the march achieved international publicity, and
encouraged unemployed miners in the Ruhr to similar action.

The march had a number of achievements to its credit.
Firstly, it led to the government setting up a special committee
to look into the problems of the unemployed. Although little
could be hoped for from this committee, it amounted to a
recognition of unemployment as a problem, which was not a
negligible achievement. Secondly, it probably did, as
Hannington claimed, head off further attacks on the
unemployed, since the previous year had seen a number of
attempts to worsen conditions. Perhaps most importantly, it
brought a limited degree of recognition from the TUC.
Although affiliation was denied the NUWCM, the TUC
agreed to establish a joint committee with the movement. The
unemployed movement's leadership was delighted with this
progress. It was probably this which led it to take a very
optimistic view of the position as the 1922-23 march
developed. With the marchers in London, *Out Of Work*
addressed its readers in its characteristically intimate way,
more reminiscent of a private letter than of a newspaper:

> Honestly, comrades, what do you think of the fight, to date, of
> the NUWCM? We found the unemployed a collection of
> whining, mimping groups, totally un-class conscious, and
> material for blacklegging. We (that is, all of us) have given the

unemployed direction, discipline and dignity. We have made unemployment *the* national issue.[38]

The assessment was a fair one. Hannington went further in a pamphlet written soon after the event. With his well developed sense of history, he compared the march to that of Wat Tyler's followers. The marchers' critics had suggested before the event that the venture would inevitably collapse in the face of the forces ranged against them: the marchers' physical condition, the weather, the Poor Law officials, the police and the government. It had indeed been far from a foregone conclusion that these obstacles would be overcome, and our hindsight threatens to lead us to underestimate the boldness of the undertaking. Hannington himself was in no doubt that: 'The march itself will go down in history as one of the great achievements of our movement.'[39] Looking back at the event over fifty years later, Sid Elias agreed with this verdict, arguing that the march aroused greater sympathy and support from the rest of the working class than any of its successors.[40] It was certainly true that the winter of 1922-23 was a high point in the NUWCM's early history. The 'Great Hunger March' confirmed that the new movement was not, as some had suspected, an ephemeral and insignificant grouping, but rather a permanent and important part of the wider labour movement.

Notes

1 *The Communist*, 13 January 1921; *Out Of Work*, No.1.
2 Ibid.
3 *The Communist*, 13 January, 26 February 1921; *Out Of Work*, No.1.
4 *The Communist*, 12 March 1921.
5 Ibid.
6 *Out Of Work*, No.1.
7 G.D.H. Cole, *A History of the Labour Party From 1914*, London 1948, p.117.
8 *Out Of Work*, No.1.
9 15 September 1921, CAB 24/128.
10 Ibid.
11 Ibid.
12 *Out Of Work*, No.11.
13 Ibid., No.13.
14 'Proposed Date of Monster Unemployed Demonstration'. CAB 24/128.

15 *Out of Work*, No.13.
16 Ibid., No.19.
17 29 September 1921. CAB 24/128.
18 *Out Of Work*, No.13.
19 Ibid., Nos. 13 and 21.
20 H. McShane, J. Smith, *No Mean Fighter*, London 1978, pp.121-41.
21 Membership cards of NUWCM(WH/CP); *Out Of Work*, Nos. 21-25.
22 *Out Of Work*, No.4.
23 Ibid., No.23.
24 Inteview with Len Choulerton, 13 August 1985.
25 Hannington, *Unemployed Struggles*, p.49.
26 *Out Of Work*, No.27.
27 Ibid., No.28.
28 Ibid., Nos 29-31; *The Communist*, 1 April 1922.
29 L.J. Macfarlane, *The British Communist Party. Its Origin and Development Until 1929*, London 1966, p.121.
30 *Out Of Work*, Nos.29-31.
31 B.R. Mitchell, P. Deane, *Abstract of British Historical Statistics*, Cambridge 1962, p.71.
32 *Out of Work*, No.34.
33 Ibid., No.30.
34 Ibid., Nos 34,37,
35 *Daily Herald*, 21 August 1922; *Out Of Work*, No.40.
36 P. Kingsford, *The Hunger Marchers in Britain, 1920-1940*, London 1982, p.33.
37 Ibid., Chapter 2; *Out Of Work* No.40.
38 *Out Of Work*, No.48.
39 W. Hannington, *The Insurgents in London*, London 1923, Preface.
40 J. Halstead, R. Harrison and J. Stevenson, 'The Reminiscences of Sid Elias', *Bulletin* of the Society for the Study of Labour History, Spring 1979, No.38, p.40.

4

The Struggle for Survival, 1923-27

Decline

The Hunger March was in many respects the most successful campaign ever run by the unemployed movement, but this was not translated into permanent gains for the NUWCM. In fact, the movement went into an immediate and steep decline. The optimism and energy generated by mass activity could only continue for a limited period of time, and gave way to exhaustion and passivity. Hannington himself admitted at the end of 1923 that the NUWCM's organisation was uneven, and that in many parts of the country there was little or no agitation that year. But his statement held good for at least another five years. Whilst the membership of the organisation stood at around 100,000 at the end of the Hunger March, and the number of committees at just under 300, the effective membership was about one-tenth that size three years later.[1] The unemployed movement gradually shrunk to a skeleton, amounting to little more than a structure, which whilst not completely immobile at any time, kept the NUWCM alive in little more than name. This was part of a broader decline in 'direct action' within the whole working class; industrial disputes grew less and less frequent and shorter in duration as the decade progressed, interrupted only by the 1926 General Strike.

The most important factor in the new movement's quiescence over the next five years was an upturn in the labour market. Unemployment fell from over two million registered at the beginning of 1922 to about one million in the summer of 1924, and whilst it rose again in the mid-1920s, did not reach 1922 levels until the very end of the decade. It was not only a question of the members lost directly to the NUWCM who moved back into employment (very few members continued their allegiance when they were in work again). It was also a question of the psychology of the situation in that people hoped that they might get work, and this tended of course to distract them from agitation as one of the unemployed. When there was some real hope of work, the workless used their energies in looking for it; in periods such as the early and late 1920s it was quite clear that there was little prospect of work and all that could be done was to fight to improve one's position as an unemployed person.

The revival in employment had its most dramatic effects in relatively prosperous areas. The next national conference had been sited in Coventry because it was felt that the local committee there was well able to host the event, but an improvement in the motor trade meant that the committee was disintegrating even before the Conference was held.

The Coventry Conference, 1923

The third national Conference held at the Sydenham Hotel, Coventry, attracted 109 delegates, representing 74 of the movement's 261 affiliated committees. The Conference opened with reports from the national officers, in which Percy Haye drew attention to the continuing financial difficulties, which had led to a hurried change of headquarters from 28 East Road to 3 Queen's Square, and to poor attendance at the NAC before the Hunger March. Hannington criticised the failure of provincial committees to adopt the factory raid tactic, but praised the committees for building the NUWCM into a 'well-knit, disciplined organisation'. No report was given by the Women's Organiser Lillian Thring as she had resigned and been replaced by Lily Webb, a member of the CPGB. The report by Harry McShane on the movement in Scotland was most encouraging, recounting the activities of the Scots in preventing evictions during the rent strike then in progress. The 40 Scottish committees, by his account, had a high degree of co-ordination.[2]

Keen debate took place on the attitude to be taken to candidates in local and national elections, with the practice of submitting questionnaires to the candidates to test how well their politics related to the movement's demands being adopted. The movement thereby neatly sidestepped any problems which might arise from any more direct affiliation to the Labour or Communist Parties. But the keenest and most closely contested discussion also related to this issue. Hitman of the Gorbals proposed that the NUWCM form a United Front with the CPGB and all other organisations prepared to fight both for the movement's demands and for the overthrow of capitalism. He argued that the socialist aims of the NUWCM, to establish 'a system of society based upon the common ownership of the means of wealth production and distribution and the carrying on of industry on the basis of production for social use and not for personal profit' should be put into practice through the 'logical step' of joining with the 'only party' which gave expression to these aims.[3] But many delegates felt this 'logical step' to be potentially disastrous. Taylor of Edinburgh, for example, spoke against the resolution, claiming that 80 per cent of the membership would leave if the motion was carried. People would not accept 'the dictation of the Communist Party'. Many delegates (though not Hannington) spoke on this resolution, which was eventually defeated by 55 votes to 52. In due course, they were to come to appreciate the value of not being tied too tightly to the CP and its changes of policy. Hannington was to have cause to defend the NUWCM's independence despite intense pressure.

The Conference reaffirmed its commitment to the Hunger March tactic. The resolution was that 'the National Hunger March be continued', and was passed enthusiastically. After several further resolutions had been passed, and Jack Holt had made a stirring speech in conclusion, the Conference ended in a display of enthusiastic solidarity, with the delegates rising to sing 'The Red Flag'. Many of them had now to walk home, having come from committees which were too hard pressed to give them their fare.[4]

The Demise of 'Out Of Work'

Soon after the Coventry Conference had disbanded, the NUWCM's excellent national newspaper *Out Of Work* ceased publication for financial reasons. The loss of this paper was a grievous blow, and arguably one from which the movement did not recover for the rest of the decade.

First launched in March 1921, it had four pages, cost a penny and appeared fortnightly. Its editor for the first two dozen issues was Lillian Thring, who was succeeded by Jack Holt. The fifteenth issue was the first to be produced under the direction of the NAC, and brought an improvement in the paper's national coverage. Correspondence from committees began to give reports from their areas. This gave *Out Of Work* a proximity to the concerns of the workless which later papers did not approach. *Out Of Work*, the reader could feel, was not a paper *for* the unemployed but one *by* them, and this made it an excellent and effective national organiser as well as a forum for discussion. By the eighteenth edition, it already claimed a circulation of sixty thousand. Because of this wide circulation, it was also a crucial contributor to democratic discussion within the unemployed movement; its loss brought crucial and disastrous closure of a major opportunity for the rank and file of the NUWCM to express itself. In terms of advocacy of the unemployed, the end of *Out Of Work* was equally damaging because, since the summer of 1922, the *Daily Herald*, the great national supporter of the movement, had come under the direct control of the Labour Party and TUC, and began to distance itself from the Communist-led NUWCM.[5]

Out Of Work had failed for financial reasons: copies were given away, one edition was read by several readers, and consequently insufficient funds were returned to the centre to pay the printer's bills. These problems were intractable, and simply moving from printer to printer in search of a new start was insufficient to overcome them. Nevertheless, the leadership made several attempts to re-launch a national newspaper. *New Charter*, an immediate successor to *Out Of Work*, soon failed, as did the *Unemployed Worker* published in the run-up to the General Election of 1924 and *Unemployed News* (first published in December 1928). From 1923 onwards, although local papers were published, the unemployed had to rely primarily on the Communist press (which the majority did not read) and internal circulars (which hardly encouraged feedback).

Subscriptions and Contact With Members

From shortly after its foundation until the late 1920s, the unemployed movement was, like its members, in a state of permanent financial crisis. The penury appears to have been especially deep between 1923 and 1927, as members moved into employment or relapsed into apathy and stopped paying their subscriptions. In the earliest days, subscriptions had often not been demanded, and systematic records were clearly lacking in many localities. People were caught up in a demonstration or meeting, gave an initial sub, and then lost contact with the movement. The Bermondsey committee, for example, was reported in early 1923 to have only 10 per cent of its nominal membership paying subs.[6] Many other committees were in a similar position. The results of this problem were twofold: to make it difficult to sustain a national structure and to create a situation in which committees substantially lost contact with their nominal members. The second consequence was at least as serious as the first, because in a period of quiescence it would have been possible to keep in touch with people through a number of methods such as circulars and meetings, but these would have had to be based on good up-to-date documentation. Without this, the task of communication was made very much more difficult.

The movement had to learn some lessons about financial arrangements through bitter experience. Initially there were quite a few cases of local treasurers embezzling or simply disappearing with the funds. Harry Young, a full-time Communist Party organiser at the time, recalls:

> As soon as they got the money they appointed a Treasurer and then the trouble started. I mean, it was some poor sod who was practically starving, had nothing to eat for a couple of days, and then they'd hand him a pound, a couple of pounds to look after, so of course there was constant trouble. They had no legal redress.[7]

Such problems were especially acute in these early years when absolute poverty was even more common than later. This was also a problem in trade unions, but more easily detected, as methods of record-keeping and financial control were better developed. An attempt to overcome this difficulty was made by introducing a rule that, wherever possible, an employed member should take on the treasurer's job, but there were still cases of funds disappearing in the 1930s.[8]

A Left Rival: The Unemployed Workers' Organisation

With the NUWCM in a difficult phase, a rival organisation emerged in London. This body grew directly out of the idea held by Sylvia Pankhurst and some of her close comrades that the NUWCM was dying because it was dominated by the CPGB. In the early autumn of 1923, Sylvia wrote to a friend saying that the new organisation, the Unemployed Workers' Organisation, would be a lively body, conducting continuous agitation and not a dead one like the NUWCM, which waited for leads from Hannington and the Communist Party. It would, she continued, revive the agitational methods of the suffragettes, and thereby displace the NUWCM as the premier unemployed movement.[9] The UWO was formed when the NUWCM's London Organiser, Harry Soderberg, defected to set it up. By late September 1923, it claimed to have 1,490 members, which would have made it approximately the same size as the NUWCM in London at that time. Its members were concentrated mainly in Bow and Poplar. Soderberg had a vision similar to Pankhurst's, of a fighting, non-bureaucratic force, and at the Coventry Conference had opposed the payment of NUWCM officials.[10]

The UWO's manifesto was presented on the front of the *Workers' Dreadnought*, Sylvia Pankhurst's paper. It adopted the 'Revolutionary watchword, abolition of the wages system', as opposed to the 'conservative slogan' of 'work or full maintenance'. The manifesto called for direct action, and in its constitution guaranteed full autonomy to each branch. The NUWCM was held to be an undemocratic body which made alliances with reformists to the detriment of the unemployed.[11] Their denunciation of the United Front strategy meant that the UWO had to face the united opposition of the NUWCM and their Labour Party allies, in particular, the Poplar Guardians. The UWO was set on a collision course with its larger opponents.

During the summer of 1923, the UWO's politics appear not to have been known to the Poplar Labour Party, as they took over an office in Poplar Town Hall, previously occupied by the NUWCM.[12] Their politics soon became apparent as the Guardians were forced to consider cutting relief due to government pressure on the funds. On 6 September, the latent conflict became a very material reality. A demonstration was held at the Guardians' meeting demanding a minimum benefit of £1 per week per adult and the restoration of coal allowances.[13] The demands were rejected, and Edgar Lansbury (George's son, a Guardian and a Communist Party member) reminded the deputation that the Guardians were actually meeting to discuss a reduction. The demonstrators then locked the doors and told the Guardians that they would stay there until the demands were met. After an hour, the Guardians called the police, who, when they arrived, refused to force an entry without written permission. Lansbury told them that he did not object to their forcing the doors, but he apparently did object (unlike the majority of the Guardians) to their entering the building. The police broke in and attacked the hundreds of demonstrators with great ferocity. The *Workers' Dreadnought* printed a list of about 30 injured, some of whom were seriously hurt. Most of them were middle-aged manual workers from local industry. A Poplar woman wrote in to say that George Lansbury had always told them to make themselves a nuisance, and this was what they found when they followed his suggestion. The paper was quick to make political points about the savage assault. This, they concluded, was what the Poplar Guardians stood for: setting the police on the workless.[14]

The police attack had its effect on the UWO's support, and the organisation faded rapidly from the scene. The majority of Poplar unemployed were well aware that, even with cuts, they were better off than their counterparts almost anywhere else in Britain. The NUWCM again stood alone as the only organisation of unemployed with any pretensions to being a national representative body, since despite its London base the UWO had some members in Scotland and aimed at becoming a national organisation. To this extent the NUWCM was, it could be argued, better off for the end of the UWO. But the argument, advanced at the time by *Workers' Dreadnought*, that the NUWCM connived at the destruction of the UWO, missed the rather more central point that the split between the Pankhurstites and the CPGB was the original and larger tragedy. The critical point had been reached when the UWO was being formed, because it was then that the experience and energies of those involved had been lost to the NUWCM.

Rivals of the Right

Although the NUWCM's only rival to its left had been extinguished, the movement still had rivals for the allegiance of the unemployed in some towns. Both the Labour Party and the Independent Labour Party (ILP) led some unemployed associations, some of which seem to have been effective advocates of the interests of the unemployed. In Bristol, Labour members of the Trades Council and then Labour MPs seized the leadership of the workless from the NUWCM at around this time. An unemployed association was established, which was given the right to individual representation to the Guardians on condition that there were no more demonstrations. During the 1924 Labour government, the Labour MPs were successful in prosecuting cases of disqualification from benefit.[15] In Reading, Alonzo Quelch, brother of the leading Communist Harry Quelch, continued to argue the cause of the unemployed as he had since he was a young member of the SDF in the 1880s. Now a member of the Board of Guardians, he refused to propose the NUWCM's scales of relief on the Board. He explained the situation:

> I had copies of the scale they wanted proposed and the rates of wages paid to the highest paid craftsmen in town. I proved by that means that their proposed scale would give to the unemployed man a bigger weekly income than the highest paid craftsman. This was an impossible scale to get and to move it would prevent us from getting the existing scale improved. Then the flattery turned to threats about what would happen to me if I still refused to move their scale. These threats they endeavoured to carry out as the weeks went by, but the scale was not moved on the Board because of its impossible character.[16]

Quelch, together with the excellent organiser Arthur Lockwood, was nevertheless at the head of protest against the scales, organising many meetings and demonstrations.[17] The

ILP set up a few unemployed associations during 1924, as part of its drive during that year to pressurise the government to take the unemployment issue more seriously. Possibly due to vigorous opposition from the NUWCM, the ILP failed to establish any national body.[18]

In a number of towns, then, the NUWCM was not the only nor even the most important organisation of unemployed. This became particularly apparent in the mid-1920s when the Communist-led movement went through a difficult period and lost many committees. But its great asset remained its already well known National Organiser, Wal Hannington, and his considerable reputation among the unemployed.

The First Labour Government, 1924 ·

Hannington had been in the Soviet Union between May and September 1923, reporting to the Second Congress of the Red International of Labour Unions on the work of the NUWCM. On his return, he led the NAC into a national campaign to revive the movement while he personally concentrated on setting the London organisation to rights. After a 'Call to Action' from the NAC at the end of September, a wide variety of work including recruitment drives, resistance to evictions and anti-emigration propaganda was begun in the localities. Emigration was to be the central theme for the winter. The approach was to be largely educational: bringing home the sometimes hard realities of life in the Dominions with information provided by the Canadian unemployed movement and others. The arguments, as Hannington expounded them to demonstrators, were simple. Vast tracts of Britain were wasting away due to lack of cultivation. Why should people unemployed through no fault of their own be shipped off to an uncertain future, losing their ties with family and friends? The country was theirs, and they should not be pressurised into leaving because the system had failed them. The leaders of the NUWCM pointed to 'model' action being taken by Scottish members in September who were then propagandising among 4,000 emigrants leaving for Canada on ships lying in the Clyde.[19] This agitation was not developed into the widespread campaign that the leadership hoped for, however, largely because of its propagandistic nature which did not relate directly to the material interests of the majority of the unemployed. Moreover, emigrants were generally identified when they had been through the government's taxing system for claiming official assistance, and had therefore already taken a firm decision.

The emigration issue was one with a certain emotive appeal in a general political sense, and therefore was more valuable as a weapon with which to attack the government. It was one part of the unemployment question which helped the Labour Party to power for the first time in the General Election. The NUWCM worked hard for the Labour candidates, and Hannington later claimed that the unemployed, through their tireless work, had made a number of Labour MPs.[20] The London District Council organised a sizeable demonstration against the 'capitalist candidates' in collaboration with the London Trades Council. Hannington, in his best oratorical style, flayed the Tory government as the government of 'Death and Disease.'[21]

The return of a Labour majority, albeit one which required support from the Liberals to form a government, awakened tremendous expectations within the working class that are difficult to recapture today. After a quarter of a century of independent political activity, the first government which could claim to represent directly working people was being formed. The labour movement as a whole had fought long and hard for political power, and felt that they had now achieved it. Hopes were high. When the new Labour MPs went off to the first session of the new Parliament, they were given rousing send-offs. The East End MPs were escorted to the House by long columns from their constituencies, within which there were strong contingents of workless, their NUWCM banners flying, cheering as their representatives left them. Would an unemployed movement be needed at all, now that the Labour Party, pledged to a programme of public works and 'work or maintenance', had arrived? The Communist leadership of the movement answered in the affirmative, but many members were unsure.

The period of the Labour government did, in fact, lead to an improvement in the situation of the unemployed. The number out of work declined from more than 1,250,000 at the end of 1923, to just over 1,000,000 by the end of July 1924.[22]

Important steps were taken to improve the lot of those still out of work. Single people living with relatives, married women, short-time workers and foreigners had the right to claim uncovenanted benefit for the first time; the period of insurance benefit was extended from 26 to 41 weeks; the 'gap' of three weeks after receiving twelve weeks' unemployment pay was ended; weekly rates were increased for men, women and dependent children.[23] These were considerable improvements. The NUWCM was not satisfied with them. In the case of the rise in 'dole', they argued that the real benefit to the unemployed could be non-existent because of the 'put-and-take' process whereby the extra money paid by the government was simply deducted again by the Guardians from payments to those receiving relief from them. The increase was not entirely pointless, however, because 'put and take' was not universally applied.

Although NUWCM activists criticised aspects of the Labour government's performance, such as its failure to prevent widespread evictions, restrictions on local authority spending and police surveillance of unemployed leaders, the majority of the unemployed did not experience these things as direct and obvious attacks on themselves. Even in the case of a very unfavourable clause in the Unemployment Insurance Bill, there was no reaction from the unemployed, nor from the NUWCM. The clause in question was 'Not Genuinely Seeking Work', which allowed benefit to be refused if it was felt that the claimant was not really looking for work. Introduced as a 'trade-off' for increased benefits, it was not seen as a major threat by the unemployed, because it was thought that it was 'only' to apply to married women. In reality, it was to be used against all claimants, irrespective of gender. The NUWCM, having lost its link with the *Workers' Dreadnought* and the Pankhurst group, was less alive to the threat than it might have been had they been in the NUWCM advocating the cause of women and pointing out the senses in which 'Not Genuinely Seeking Work' was a threat to all the unemployed. It was not until 1927 that the movement, realising the large numbers being disqualified under this clause, began to make an issue of it.

Relations with the TUC

The TUC had agreed to form a joint committee with the
NUWCM at the height of the Hunger Marchers' agitation in
London in January 1923. But from that point onwards, the
TUC gradually back-tracked, with unfortunate consequences
for the unemployed movement. This was largely because the
circumstances of trade union leaders changed considerably
from early 1923 onwards. Initially, the trade unions had
greatly feared losing the allegiance of their unemployed
members as they ceased paying out union unemployment
benefit, and were worried about the possibility of these
ex-members forming a pool of labour which could force down
earnings through mass scabbing. As the NUWCM seemed to
be developing into a genuinely representative organisation of
workless, the best option seemed to be that of establishing a
form of co-operation which could bring the NUWCM into the
TUC's sphere of influence without actually committing the
TUC to anything in particular. But it soon became apparent
that the interests of trade union leaders were not as threatened
as they had thought. The unions became increasingly stable
as institutions as they successfully raised contributions so as to
guarantee a much larger income to their head offices.
Throughout the 1920s, income to national offices was never
less than (and generally considerably more than) double the
figure for 1914.[24] Mass scabbing had not taken place and after
an initial bout of wage-cutting, wage rates remained stable for
the remainder of the decade. The lack of widespread
strike-breaking had of course in part been due to the activities
of the NUWCM, and in this sense the movement had defeated
itself. But more importantly, the TUC could see that as
individual unions were recovering, the NUWCM was
faltering. The anticipated sustained, large-scale movement of
unemployed had not materialised. Within a year of the end of
the Hunger March, the only impulse driving the TUC
towards collaboration with the NUWCM was its rather weak
general sense of social concern, and so the balance of forces
was very much in the trade unions' favour.

When the TUC agreed to form a Joint Advisory Committee
(JAC), it laid down terms for the operation of that body which
it refused to discuss with the NUWCM. These were to be that

the function of the Committee would be to advise the General Council; it would not be able to initiate action, nor to make statements without the General Council's approval. The JAC would be allowed to form local equivalents, an important opportunity that does not seem to have been followed up.[25] The JAC first met one year after the initial discussions, with the Labour government in power. Ben Tillett headed the TUC side, with Finlay and Bramley. Holt, Haye and Straker attended for the NUWCM. Hannington was absent due to illness, despite his later assertion to the contrary.[26] The central result of the first meeting was a joint programme of demands called the Unemployed Charter:

We demand:
1. Work or effective maintenance for all unemployed workers and increased government assistance to be provided through trade unions. All unemployment relief to be completely dissociated from Poor Law administration.
2. The immediate development of government schemes of employment to absorb the unemployed in their own trades at trade union rates of wages and conditions.
3. The establishment of state workshops for the purpose of supplying the necessary services or commodities to meet the requirements of government departments.
4. The reduction in the hours of labour necessary to absorb unemployed workers, the normal working day or week to be regulated by the requirements of the industry.
5. The establishment of occupational training centres for unemployed workers, providing proper training with effective maintenance, particularly for unemployed boys and girls and able-bodied ex-servicemen.
6. The provision of suitable housing accomodation at rents within the means of wage-earners, and the proper use of existing houses.[27]

Hannington acclaimed the Charter as 'a new stage in the unemployed struggle', telling critics within the movement who pointed to its mildness and failure to make proposals for action that a week of agitation was to take place beginning on 24 May 1924. These demonstrations turned out to be a failure, despite Hannington's claim to the contrary in *Unemployed Struggles*, in which he confuses them with rather better turnouts in 1925.[28] Only just over 1,000 programmes were sold for the final demonstration on Sunday 1 June and a total of £8 was collected. The underlying reason for the poor showing was, in several senses, the Labour government. The TUC had not mobilised unions because it did not wish to embarrass the government, whilst the unemployed were largely satisfied by benefit increases.

Just two months later, at the founding conference of the Communist organisation within the trade unions, the Minority Movement, Hannington expanded on the 'considerable importance' of the JAC. But the formation of the Minority Movement (MM), which pledged itself to the 'closest possible relationship' with the NUWCM, made the TUC more nervous of the JAC. The MM sought to group all militant individuals within the unions, and to organise them so as to 'ginger' the existing leaderships into more militant policies. With Hannington himself elected as the first secretary of the Metalworkers' MM, the TUC leaders became even more frightened of the Communist Party generally, since it was now actively organising employed workers in the trade unions.[29] Thus, although the General Council agreed to demonstrations in June 1921, and these were moderately successful, the TUC was upset by critical remarks made by some speakers. The following month, the TUC held a special Conference on unemployment, at which Hannington addressed the TUC Conference for the last time. Openly deriding the prepared resolutions, Hannington called them 'hardy annuals' and called for a definite plan of action. If the General Council refused, then they would mark themselves out as 'men and women with a streak of cowardice, afraid to face the responsibilities that lay before them'.[30] This was too much for the General Council, who rejected the next request of the JAC for a speaker at Conference.[31] The recriminations following the General Strike brought the end of the JAC.

A Local Campaign: Clydebank

Whilst the Labour government had generally dampened the level of unemployed struggles, it did allow the TUC to feel free to campaign with the NUWCM, albeit in a limited way. The government also gave hope to those fighting evictions, by introducing Wheatley's Anti-Eviction Bill. Major battles took place on this issue, showing that the unemployed movement was still alive and active, and that although the national picture was bleak, the local position was sometimes rather more hopeful.

The 1915 Clydeside rent strike had forced the government to freeze rents at their 1914 level, and although the 1920 Rent and Mortgage Interest Act allowed rents to be increased if improvements were carried out, tenants from all over Scotland resolved in 1920 to pay only the 1914 rent. The Scottish landlords were enraged by this decision, and carried out retaliatory evictions on a large scale during the early post-war years. In these years, upwards of thirty thousand applications for possession were being made annually throughout Britain, and the indications are that in Scotland at least the rate of evictions increased dramatically during 1924.[32] It was in Clydebank that resistance was strongest: a history of labour movement concern with housing issues and the homogeneity of the community combined to create strong opposition to evictions. But the issue was of national importance. Evictions affected the position of the unemployed more than any other single factor: without housing, people were truly in dire straits. Hannington recognised the importance of the housing question. After the defeat of Wheatley's Anti-Eviction Bill in the House of Commons in the spring of 1924, Hannington argued that now the movement's slogan would have to be: 'Evictions Must Stop!'[33] Wheatley's Bill had certainly raised the hopes of tenants throughout Britain. Its defeat encouraged the Scottish landlords to increase the tempo of evictions still further. The stakes had been raised hugely during 1924.

In Clydebank, the storm centre of the eviction battle, there were two main schools of thought on how best to resist. The most important was represented by Andrew Leiper, the local representative of the ILP-led Scottish Housing Association. Leiper had brilliantly exploited the legal possibilities of the situation. In November 1920, the Housing Association had won a judgement that all rent above the 1914 level had to be repaid to tenants as from 1915; this major step forward encouraged many more people to join the rent 'strike'. When evictions started to increase, the Housing Association also succeeded in establishing that the vast majority of evictions were unlawful because no 'notice of removal' (required by

Scottish law) had been served on the tenants. The decision was contested up to the House of Lords, where the Association's arguments were finally upheld in November 1922.[34] Clearly, Leiper and the Housing Association could claim great success for their approach, at least until May 1925, when the Constable Commission recommended changes in the law which removed many of the tenants' rights. The other school of thought, led by the unemployed committee, held that such changes were bound to arrive, but, more importantly, drew attention to the fact that despite these judgements, people were still being put into the street. The essential point, they contended, was to take direct action to prevent evictions whilst calling on the labour movement for support. The legal approach was not ruled out by the unemployed committee, it was simply considered inadequate.

The NUWCM locally had been swollen by its readiness to respond in this way. The unemployed could very often not afford to pay 1914 rents (which in Clydebank were relatively high), and so the NUWCM's tactics were very appropriate. Time after time, at the local meetings held to discuss the best way forward, the unemployed committee's tribune, Jimmy McCafferty, rose to argue that direct action had to be combined with an appeal to the labour movement to defend them.[35] These speeches reflected the committee's activity in the streets. Mr Gillespie told Sean Damer:

> So the NUWM, the National Unemployed Workers' Movement – it was hell of an active – they were the driving force. The Rent Strike would never have become known unless for the NUWM. Andrew Leiper was looking after the administrative side, and we were in the NUWM. So we decided tae look after the other side. People were getting evicted and we decided tae stop the evictions. Of course, we knew we couldnae stop them, but what we did was – oh, we'd a great movement – the shopkeepers gave us free grub, beef and all the rest of it, and a lot of Labour women, they cooked the grub in the ILP rooms, and we sent out an SOS for bikes. The bicycles came pouring in, so we formed a bicycle patrol. They patrolled the boundary and when any Sheriff officer – well there werenae too many motor cars on the road then – and when the Sheriff's officer came in the bloke cycled down to us over here. We got to know who they were going to evict, so crowds gathered in the place, filled up the closes, went

into the houses, barricaded them up and the Sheriff's officers had tae retire, and they had a police escort. But some people *were* evicted that couldnae pay any rent. It was a Labour Town Council – a Labour government and a Labour Town Council. So the Labour Town Council, they didnae want to defy Ramsay's crowd. [i.e. Ramsay MacDonald, R.C.] you see, but they were terrible sympathetic towards us. So some of the people who were evicted – we persuaded the council tae give them tents and it was bloody freezing and the men and women were in them. So I went back to the Council again and persuaded them tae buy railway carriages. Well, they bought the railway carriages and the people were kind of more sheltered.[36]

His testimony demonstrates yet again that concern with the immediate material needs of the workless which characterised the NUWCM. By their tenacious solidarity, they received some minimal comfort for those previously abandoned by the authorities.

The defeat of the Wheatley Bill, and the report of the Constable Commission meant that, by the end of 1925, the terms of the battle had shifted decisively towards the landlords. The earlier success of the legal tactic had now become a major liability as the law gradually became more favourable to the factors. The Sheriff's officers saw their way clear to adopting increasingly brutal methods in evictions. Whilst the community had adopted the technique of 'moving' when an eviction threatened so that the tenant was not the person named on the eviction decree, the Sheriff's officers now began to remove the doors and window frames of both the tenant's house and the house to which the tenant had 'moved'.[37] The results of this illegal tactic in the Scottish winter are not hard to imagine: solidarity between tenants was stretched to breaking point. Meanwhile, the unemployed committee was having to fight on another front as relief had been reduced by the Parish Council.[38] The tenants were in headlong retreat. For the rest of the decade, the unemployed committee continued to lead demonstrations with their band at evictions, but effective resistance had been ended.

The 1924 and 1925 National Conferences: Survival the Objective

The 1924 National Conference met in Sheffield on 6 December 1924. The Labour government had fallen, victim of the so-called 'Zinoviev Letter', which had been publicised as carrying 'instructions' from the Communist International to the Labour Party. Yet the Communism of the delegates was proudly and defiantly paraded in a more open way than previously, even though there were only 44 of them. Many delegates wore the Soviet star on their lapels, and even their evening recreation consisted of a 'proletarian concert' by Arnold Freeman.[39]

Percy Haye detailed the difficulties facing the movement: serious financial worries had been compounded by the complete failure of the NAC to function at all. There were about two dozen active committees. Hannington, whilst careful to begin by spiriting the delegates away to the red flags and revolutionary optimism of the Soviet Union, soon came back to Britain and criticised the lack of response to headquarters circulars and the absence of 'solid work locally'. The problem was clearly one of ensuring the continued existence of the movement. Various solutions were adopted: the cost of membership was increased from one to two pence, employed people were to be admitted to the NUWCM for the first time, and anyone thirteen weeks in arrears would be considered no longer a member.[40] One possible widening of the movement's base was rejected, as a proposed women's conference was turned down, and women's participation continued to decline until the end of the decade.

A new headquarters sub-committee was elected by Conference to determine policy between NACs. The committee consisted of the national officials, plus three people elected by the Conference.[41] Here was a serious step away from democracy, made necessary by the difficulty of getting a functioning NAC. The NAC had become nothing more than a notional leadership. Yet, if the movement was to survive, some direction was needed. The officials were, in effect to become the leadership. They now had better office facilities, at 105 Hatton Gardens, further expanding the possibilities of running an adequate national office. The problem may be illustrated by looking at the position with Hannington, who had increasingly involved himself in the Metalworkers' Minority Movement and other Communist Party work since mid-1924. Although his non-NUWCM work was criticised at the 1926 Conference, how could his activities be monitored? The Conference obviously could not ascertain just how much time Hannington was spending on outside work, whilst the headquarters sub-committee could not deal with a leader of such standing. Over the next few years, the work and very existence of the NUWCM lay in the hands of national officials, and that in large part meant in the hands of Wal Hannington. It was fortunate that they were so able. But patterns of decision-making were being set which were eroding the democratic process within the NUWCM. The movement was surviving, but in an attenuated and ossified form.

The 1925 Conference, held in Stoke, provided more grounds for optimism than the Sheffield Conference. More than twice the number of delegates attended partly because of a Communist Party decision to strengthen its work among the unemployed, and partly because the movement had benefited from the establishment of Councils of Action throughout Britain to support the miners when the expected conflict broke out over the anticipated end to the government subsidy to the coalowners. Once again, the unemployed movement had benefited from an upturn of activity amongst employed workers. Hannington, however, was not present at the Conference, having been imprisoned along with many other Communist leaders, and was therefore restricted to sending an encouraging letter to the delegates.[42]

Reports received gave the strong impression of growing membership and activity in the coalmining areas. But this in itself gave rise to a problem in South Wales which was to be significant throughout the movement's life. Jack Thomas, Assistant National Organiser, explained that the context was different in South Wales because the South Wales Miners' Federation (SWMF) was the only major trade union to take the organisation of unemployed members seriously.

Unemployed miners were encouraged to retain involvement in their lodges, and this had begun to mean that some lodges were becoming preoccupied with unemployed problems. In

Dowlais and Merthyr, S.O. Davies instituted a scheme whereby the unemployed miners paid a penny a week into a special sub-committee within the lodge whose specific function was to represent the unemployed and to agitate on their behalf. Davies had already been involved in a discussion with Hannington on this issue in the *Sunday Worker*, and argued that the unity of the labour movement would be best served by his strategy, while Hannington replied that the consequence would be to divide the unemployed of Britain according to their trade union. The NUWCM, Hannington had stated, was in favour of the unemployed staying in their unions, but was also for an independent organisation which would more accurately reflect the concerns of the unemployed. Hannington argued along lines which still have considerable relevance today. Whilst being careful not to accuse the unions of neglecting their responsibilities to out-of-work members, he was insistent that only an organisation *of* the workless could hope adequately to pursue their interests. The leaders of the NUWCM were faced with a peculiar situation in South Wales, where their arguments appeared to have had less force because of the position of 'the Fed' as the only significant union in the coalfields. This could present itself as a problem on occasions when the union claimed rights as the sole organiser of the unemployed miners in South Wales. The area was an important one for the unemployed movement, and could not simply be written off to the SWMF, whose attitude to the NUWCM was not at this point entirely friendly.

Jack Thomas reported that the difficulty remained in Dowlais, where the NUWCM had been unable to 'get a hold'. The Conference went into secret session for this debate, in which the need for the unemployed movement was reasserted. But the difficulty, which lay primarily outside the NUWCM, remained.[43] Here was another threat to the existence of the movement, which was to resurface a decade later.

The elections held at the end of the Conference confirmed Hannington in his pre-eminent position within the movement. His importance having been recognised by the state, which had imprisoned him, it was confirmed by the Conference. He had already become a heroic figure in the minds of many activists, and was re-elected National Organiser unopposed and to 'a storm of applause'. The other key posts were retained by those who held them, with Mrs Barton filling the vacant and unenviable position of Women's Organiser.[44] The Conference ended with Jack Holt reminding everyone of the vital role that the NUWCM would have to play in the industrial struggle that undoubtedly lay ahead. The 'Blackleg-Proof' badge that everyone wore would have to be lived up to. As 'The Internationale' was sung before dispersal, the chorus, with its reference to the final struggle about to begin, must have carried a more direct significance than usual. The day of reckoning was not far off; here was the call to arms.

The General Strike and Its Aftermath

As the General Strike approached, the NUWCM constantly linked the struggles of the employed and unemployed. A large demonstration which took place in the spring of 1926 in Porth, South Wales, was a typical example. Processions from Tonyrefail, Llynypia, the Rhondda Fach and Upper Rhondda converged on Porth on a Sunday afternoon in protest at a reduction in unemployed relief by the Pontypridd Guardians. The Rhondda Fach contingent started off in Mardy (where there was a strong unemployed committee) with 400 men and 100 women, their silver band at the front. As the procession wound through the continuous band of scarcely separated pit villages, it grew until it was half a mile long. Tylorstown's banner was revealing, depicting as it did a wartime scene with a wounded soldier adjacent to another tableau showing the same soldier begging for a job. Other banners carried slogans: 'All Power to the Workers', 'Death Before Starvation'. In Porth, the large crowd was addressed by the fiery Mardy Communist Arthur Horner, who proposed resolutions calling for restoration of the old scales of relief, and for the Miners' Federation and TUC to resist any attempt to increase miners' hours or reduce their pay. Horner stressed the link between the two issues: the mining communities were under attack by the class enemy, and had to be met with a united response.[45]

The NUWCM played its part in the General Strike of 1926. In many areas, unemployed delegates sat on strike committees, and many local studies pay tribute to the part that they played in trying to prevent strike-breaking.[46] During the strike, the developing confrontation between the government and certain Labour-dominated Boards of Guardians came to a head. The Cabinet clearly took a very dim view of Guardians supporting miners and strikes. The government decided simply to remove the elected Guardians and to replace them by Commissioners responsible directly to government. The pretext for removing the Guardians was that they had run up debts by providing relief at relatively high rates, often without any repayment conditions. Under the Board of Guardians (Default) Act of July 1926, Commissioners replaced the Guardians at Birtley (Chester-le-Street Union), West Ham and Bedwellty. The Commissioners quickly set about manufacturing retrospective justification for their appointment. In Birtley, they found that the Labour Guardians had been supported during the strike by collections organised by the local NUWCM. Preferring not to put themselves at the mercy of hostile Relieving Officers, the Labour Guardians subsisted on the money which the unemployed movement could collect for them. But, even worse than their association with the NUWCM was their trade union 'coercion'. They had for some time refused to allow Relieving Officers to pay relief to anyone not in possession of an up-to-date union card. The reaction of the Commissioners can be imagined. They were apoplectic. Yet, scandalised as they clearly were, they found it difficult to establish breach of any statute and therefore recommended that the Guardians be charged with conspiracy to defraud the Ministry of Health.[47] The Commissioners in the three Poor Law Unions saw it as their duty to slash benefit in their areas. In Bedwellty, the Guardians, pushed into massive debt by the miners' strike, were superseded by one Major Dixon, whose barbarous activities revolved around the simple expedient of virtually abolishing relief. In December 1926, the cost of relief in the area was £13,268; one year later, it was £1,146.[48] The NUWCM in Bedwellty worked closely with the miners' lodges to urge people not to repay relief paid out on loan during the strike. They were cutting with the grain in any case, because most people simply could not pay. Whilst the NUWCM argued on the streets, from house to house, the Labour

ex-Guardians joined with them. Meanwhile, the miners'
lodges prevented illegal deductions from pay attempted by the
coalowners at the behest of Major Dixon. The Commissioners
tried to obtain court orders, but complained of the
effectiveness of the oppositional movement.[49]

For the government, the Commissioners' investigations
confirmed their suspicions about the links between the
NUWCM, some Guardians and the 1926 strikers. The defeat
of the General Strike and the apparent success of the
Commisioners in curbing 'profligacy' gave them the
opportunity to propose radical reforms to the way that benefit
was administered. Chamberlain's proposal to abolish the
Guardians altogether had been seen as too radical before the
General Strike: large numbers of middle-class people were
involved in the system and would resent the loss of power
involved.[50] After the strike, such a change, though still disliked
by some, became more acceptable. Having symbolically
defeated the industrial wing of the labour movement, the
Conservatives felt confident to proceed with an attack on their
poor but troublesome cousins, the unemployed.

Defending the Guardians? The Labour Party and the NUWCM

The government proposals were embodied in the Poor Law
Reform Bill and entailed abolition of the Boards of Guardians
and the administration of relief finance by County Councils.
This was largely designed to remove the point of
administration further away from the locality, so as to reduce
the possibilities for exerting local pressure on the Guardians.
But it also had the immediate effect of dividing the NUWCM
and the Labour Party.

The Labour Party's Special Conference of April 1926 had
approved reform of the Poor Law system and was in favour of
transferring the Guardians' duties to local councils. Although
their proposals were not the same as those being made by the
Conservatives, they were in this respect quite close. The
NUWCM, on the other hand, took the position that the Bill
should be withdrawn, and a campaign begun to extend the
powers of the Guardians. In line with their policy of raising
the finance for benefit on a national level, they also argued

that more money should be raised for the Guardians through higher rates of tax on upper-income earners.[51]

The disagreement with the Labour Party gave rise to considerable debate within the unemployed movement as to which policy was in fact best. The national leadership argued that abolition of the Guardians would undermine their ability to put pressure on the Guardians. But there were many in the NUWCM who could not find it in themselves to campaign for the retention of the hated 'Guardians of the Rates'. Strong emotions were aroused; one correspondent to the Communist *Workers' Weekly* incredulously inquired since when the NUWCM had been in favour of the Poor Law? Surely they did not really propose defending those who were grinding the faces of the workless into the dust? The same correspondent also pointed out that if relief finance was to be raised on a county basis, then that would be to the good because one of the demands of the Poplar Guardians, namely that the better-off districts would subsidise the worse-off would be conceded. *Workers' Weekly*'s editor scorned this last idea, suggesting that nothing of the sort would happen, but he could not deny the deep feeling that many people had against the Guardians. For many years, the Guardians had been the enemy despite the capture of a few local Boards by the Labour Party. Why not tear the whole system down? It was no use, the correspondent argued, simply adopting a traditionalist, negative stance: if the Poor Law needed reforming, then it should be done, even if it was the Tories who did it.[52] These debates meant that there was no massive campaign to defend the Guardians when they were abolished in 1929. Such limited opposition as there was came mainly from Guardians themselves, and it is misleading to suggest as some historians have done, that there was any real popular base to the protests. In fact, in this sense the government's strategy had worked very well indeed.[53]

The Blanesburgh Report

If the Poor Law Reform Bill split the Labour Party and the NUWCM, the report of the Blanesburgh committee in 1927 was to cause a decisive break with the TUC. The committee had long been the subject of warnings from Hannington, who

was an assiduous student of official thinking. In his view, soon
to be proven substantially correct, the report would be the
basis for a new Bill, under which extended benefit (for those
who had exhausted their entitlement to the standard
six-month entitlement) would be replaced by a 'transitional'
benefit. Although claimants would have a statutory right to
the new benefit, he or she would have to have made 30
contributions in the previous two years, a much higher
requirement than before. After thirteen weeks, the person's
contributions record would again be scrutinised and, to be
entitled to further benefit, this record would still have to show
30 contributions. These provisions hit the many workers in
seasonal trades, whose contribution records were necessarily
intermittent, particularly hard. Even worse, the rates for adult
men and young people were to be reduced, whilst the 'Not
Genuinely Seeking Work' clause was to be 'tightened' in
several important respects. The clause would be applied if
after a 'reasonable' time the claimant could not find work at
his or her trade and refused work of any sort. Concrete
evidence of positive efforts to find work could also be
required.[54] Taken as a whole, the report was probably the
most important attack on the conditions of the unemployed to
take place in the 1920s. Hannington estimated that
implementation of its recommendations would mean 250,000
people losing their benefit altogether. Moreover, because the
proposals were linked to a suggestion that the employed
should pay lower insurance contributions, they threatened to
deepen the division between those in and out of work. The
only answer to these problems, Hannington argued in his
pamphlet *The Meaning of the Blanesburgh Report*, was to
strengthen the unemployed movement by massive recruitment
to its ranks. He saw it as futile to begin by calling for Hunger
Marches and other forms of action whilst the movement
remained so weak. The NUWCM was in no position to make
an adequate answer to such an onslaught without much
expanded human resources. The report did bring a reaction
from the gradually swelling pool of unemployed, and played
some part in helping to arouse the workless from a period of
relative quiescence. The NUWCM's revival occurred in
isolation from the TUC.[55]

The Blanesburgh Report clearly dismayed Hannington and

the leaders of the NUWCM, even though they had from the beginning warned of the likelihood of its containing savage proposals. But what enraged the leadership beyond measure was the role of the TUC's representatives on the Blanesburgh Committee. The Report marked the beginning of a new tone in relations between the NUWCM and the official labour movement, in which the NUWCM began to speak in terms of incredulous bitterness about the betrayals it felt it was suffering. Vituperative criticisms were poured on the head of Margaret Bondfield, who, as TUC representative on the Blanesburgh Committee, had signed the report in what Hannington called 'a standing disgrace to them [the TUC] for all time'.[56] Since not one of the TUC's recommendations to the committee had been carried out, how, Hannington asked, could Bondfield sign it? In the eyes of the NUWCM, the Labour Party was soon made an accomplice of the TUC, when, at a special TUC-Labour Party Conference a motion from the Miners' Federation demanding complete opposition to the report and censure of the signatories was ruled out of order, and it was decided to delegate the Parliamentary Labour Party alone to fight the Bill in the House of Commons.[57] Hannington argued that the 'apathy of the official Labour Movement to this Bill' was 'truly amazing'.[58]

From the TUC and Labour Party's point of view, the strength of feeling coming from the NUWCM was predictable bluster. Both wings of the official labour movement had decided, after the General Strike, that industrial action should effectively be abandoned for the foreseeable future, and that political accommodation should be the order of the day. They saw the future largely in terms of parliamentary action, and the NUWCM as an embarrassment. The last meeting of the TUC-NUWCM Joint Advisory Committee took place in August 1926. When, in March 1927, the NUWCM asked the TUC's General Secretary, Walter Citrine, for a JAC meeting, he replied that nothing useful would come of it, and when the NUWCM then approached the General Council, it was told that the JAC was to be ended.[59] No explanation was offered until much later, in the report of the General Council to the 1928 TUC Conference, when it was explained that 'very little in the way of practical proposals' had been forthcoming from the NUWCM, and that the General Council was not satisfied as to their *bona fides*.[60] The explanations were threadbare to say the least. The NUWCM had made all the running on the JAC, only to have the JAC's proposals turned down by the General Council, whilst the question of its *bona fides* is clearly no more than a coded reference to its association with the Communist Party, a link that had been obvious from the beginning. This high-handed abolition of the JAC ushered in a new era in NUWCM-TUC relations. The NUWCM was cast into outer darkness by the TUC, which tried to isolate the unemployed movement from the rest of the labour movement at local level. It was little wonder, then, that the NUWCM began to criticise the TUC in sharp terms. So bitter was the tone of the exchanges, and so deep were the recriminations, that there could never be a return to the co-operation of 1923, which began to appear, with the advantage of hindsight, as having been a moment of profound harmony.

Such harmony had never of course existed in reality. It was only in the changed circumstances of the mid-1930s, when Hannington was trying to bring the TUC back into a working relationship, that he could say that the committee had done 'such good work'.[61] The 1929 NUWCM Conference received a much more scathing assessment from the national officials, who argued that the JAC had been a 'Mere pretence of interest by the TUC ... we were regarded more or less as a nuisance to be patronisingly tolerated but quietly curbed'.[62] This latter statement, for all its venom, was closer to the mark than Hannington's later view. But although the JAC had not done 'such good work', its *existence* had been an important support for the NUWCM, since it had allowed the movement to approach labour bodies at local level with good prospects of acceptance. This had been an important prop for the NUWCM during the difficult mid-1920s, but it had now been removed. It was fortunate for the unemployed movement that there were signs of a slight revival in its fortunes.

Notes

1 *Report* of the Third National Conference, pp.1-2.
2 Ibid, pp.1-13.
3 Ibid, pp.19-20.
4 Ibid, pp.26-7.

5 *Daily Herald*, 6 September, 25 November 1922.

6 *Out Of Work*, No.50.

7 Interview with Harry Young by Derick Newland (date unknown).

8 See, for example, S. Morgan to W. Hannington on the problems of auditing the 1934 Hunger March (J.S. Williams of Dowlais, papers, 0/ii/2/7, South Wales Coalfield Archive, University College, Swansea).

9 S. Franchini, *Sylvia Pankhurst 1912-24. Dal Suffragismo alla Rivoluzione Sociale*, Pisa 1980, pp.269-70.

10 *Report* of the Third National Conference, p.25.

11 *Workers' Dreadnought*, 7,21 July 1923.

12 Ibid.

13 Ibid., 6 October 1923.

14 Ibid., 27 September, 6 October 1923.

15 R. Whitfield, 'The Labour Movement in Bristol, 1910-1939', unpublished M. Litt. Thesis, University of Bristol, 1979, pp.200-21.

16 Alonzo Quelch, unpublished autobiography, p.7, (kindly lent me by Keith Jerrome).

17 A.Lockwood, 'The Labour Movement in Reading, 1920-29', p.15, (unpublished manuscript kindly lent me by Keith Jerrome).

18 *Daily Herald*, 20,23 June 1924. For the history of an association in Staffordshire at this time, see *Staffordshire Sentinel* 1, 14 October 1924, and *Workers' Weekly*, 3,7 October 1924.

19 *Workers' Weekly*, 28 September 1923; see also, *All Power*, August 1923.

20 *Workers' Weekly*, 28 December 1923; Hannington had already made a similar claim for the Hunger March (*The Insurgents in London*, p.6).

21 *Workers' Weekly*, 30 November 1923.

22 H.H. Tiltman, *James Ramsay MacDonald*, London 1929, p.171.

23 Ibid; see also p.172.

24 Mitchell and Deane, op.cit., pp.68-9.

25 S. Shaw, 'The Attitude of the TUC Towards Unemployment in the Inter-War Period', unpublished PhD Thesis, University of Kent, 1979, pp.309-11.

26 Ibid., p.311,n.1; *Unemployed Struggles*, p.122.

27 *All Power*, April 1924.

28 Shaw, op.cit.,p.313; *Unemployed Struggles*, p.128.

29 *Report* of the National Minority Movement Conference, 23,24 August 1924, pp.2,11-12.

30 *Minutes* of the JAC, 7 July 1925, (TUC Archive).

31 Shaw, op.cit., p.39.

32 D. Englander, 'Landlord and Tenant in Urban Britain: The Politics of Housing Reform, 1838-1924', unpublished PhD Thesis, University of Warwick, 1979, pp.437, 449, 458: *Glasgow Evening News*, 15 April 1924; *Glasgow News*, 12 April 1924.

33 *All Power*, May 1924; *Workers' Weekly*, 2 May 1924.

34 S. Damer, *Rent Strike!* Clydebank 1982, pp.1-6.

35 *Clydebank Press*, 6 February, 15 May, 19 June 1925.

36 Damer, op.cit.,p.13.

37 Ibid., p.14; *Clydebank Press*, 6 February, 15 May 1925.

38 *Clydebank Press*, 14 August 1925.

39 *Workers' Weekly*, 5 December 1924; *Sheffield Independent*, 8 December 1924.

We Refuse to Starve in Silence

40 *Report* of the Fourth National Conference, pp.2-5; *Sheffield Independent*, 8 December 1924.
41 *Report* of the Fourth National Conference, p.12.
42 J.T. Murphy, *The Political Meaning of the Great Strike*, London 1926, p.54; *Report* of the Fifth National Conference, pp.5-6
43 *Sunday Worker*, 13 September 1925; H. Francis and D. Smith, *The Fed* London 1980, pp.187-9.
44 *Report* of the Fifth National Conference, pp.31,36.
45 *Workers' Weekly*, 23 April 1926.
46 See J. Klugmann, *History of the Communist Party of Great Britain*, Vol.2: *The General Strike 1925-6*, London 1969, p.149.
47 Chester-le-Street Union, *Report* of the Board of Guardians on the Administration for the Period 30 August 1926 to 31 December 1926, Cmnd 2818, 1927, xi, pp.7,8,10,12.
48 S.R. Williams, 'The Bedwellty Board of Guardians and the Default Act of 1927', *Llafur*, Spring 1979, Vol.2, Part 4, p.74.
49 *Report* of the Board of Guardians appointed by the Ministry of Health to constitute the Board of Guardians for the Bedwellty Union, Cmnd 2976, 1927, xi, p.12.
50 K.Middlemas and J.Barnes, *Baldwin: A Biography*, London 1969, pp.454-7.
51 *Workers' Weekly*, 7 January 1926.
52 Ibid.
53 Kingsford, op.cit.,p.80.
54 *Workers' Weekly* 18 February 1927.
55 W. Hannington, *The Meaning of the Blanesburgh Report*, London 1927, pp.13-5.
56 Ibid.,p.4.
57 *Workers' Life*, 6 May 1927.
58 Ibid.
59 Ibid., 9 March 1928.
60 TUC Congress *Report* 1928, p.113.
61 *Unemployed Struggles*, p.140.
62 *Report* of the Sixth National Conference, p.12.

5

Slow Revival, 1927-30

The Welsh Miners' March

The period between the end of the miners' strike of 1926 and the Wall Street crash was one of slow revival for the unemployed movement. This was based primarily on an increase in the number of miners out of work, but a number of other circumstances were involved. Perhaps the most significant was the fact that many Communists, and especially those in the mining areas, had been sacked and had little option for the foreseeable future but to organise themselves within the NUWCM. Until 1926, coal mining had been relatively sheltered from unemployment compared to other staple industries, but after the General Strike the rate of unemployment shot up, so that by 1928 almost a quarter of the nation's mining workforce was displaced; in some areas, notably South Wales, the effective rate of unemployment was much higher. In some pit villages, the NUWCM expanded its presence considerably during this period. In Mardy, for example, the committee kept meticulous records of members' contributions, and these show a growth from 477 to 654 between March 1926 and March 1927.[1] There was a very real sense in which the miners' struggle moved out of the industrial arena and onto the streets in the decade after 1926. The pitmen led the resurgence of the unemployed movement.

The idea of a march of unemployed miners from South Wales to London came, not from the NUWCM, but from a group of South Wales miners led by Hannington's close personal friend Arthur Horner, and A.J.Cook. With the NUWCM's agreement, Horner began to organise the march. With Hannington, Horner and Cook sharing platforms, the protests of the miners in and out of work came close to being fused. Hannington stressed from the very beginning that just one cause was at stake: the cause of the whole community. The marchers demands would include not only decent relief and the dropping of the Blanesburgh-inspired Unemployment Bill, but an adequate response to the deep problems of the coal industry.[2] But the march failed to achieve the support the leaders wanted from the South Wales Miners' Federation, which had yet to be transformed by the work of Horner and other Communists.

The march consisted of 300 miners, the majority of them ex-servicemen, from the Welsh valleys to London, and took place between 8 and 27 November. The marchers had to face the prospect of having no support along the route, as the TUC had circularised Trades Councils advising them that they could not recommend giving help. Undeterred, they carried on, and in fact were greatly helped along the route wherever they stopped. Small concessions in terms of the new Unemployment Bill were won (postponement of the 30-stamp requirement for one year, and small changes in the benefit rates).[3] Hannington, in his twopenny pamphlet *The March of the Miners. How We Smashed the Opposition,* gave a racy description of the trek in a fine demonstration of the pamphleteer's art, which showed the way in which the TUC's circular was swept aside.

The Welsh miners' march was also the occasion for the CPGB and the NUWCM to publicise its activities to the rest of the international Communist movement. The stock of the CPGB had not been high with the Communist International for some time, and the miners' march was an opportunity for the CPGB to raise its standing somewhat, because it appeared to fit in well with the new policies then being launched within the International. Essentially, the previous tactics of the 'United Front' with reformist organisations were being abandoned in favour of direct confrontation with the reformists. The analysis was that international capital had now entered its 'Third Period' since the October Revolution, one in which it was in acute crisis. All that stood between the working class and socialist revolution were leaders of the Labour Party-TUC type. All ideas of alliance with such traitors therefore had to be abandoned: what was now required was 'independent leadership.' Workers had to be approached directly by

Communist organisations, and a 'United front built from below.' For the CPGB, the Welsh miners' march could be interpreted as fitting in quite well with the new policies, as both Arthur Horner at the Red International of Labour Unions, and Hannington at the Communist International suggested in their speeches. Horner was careful to point out that, in Britain, at least, the trade unions were not simply a tool in the hands of the capitalist class, and that they should not be surrendered to the reformist leaders. Having distanced himself from the line in this way, Horner then argued that the miners' march had shown that it was possible to build the 'united front from below'. The marchers had not waited for help from the bureaucrats, but had gone ahead with their march despite an apparent lack of preparation. The result had been strong support from the working class in all areas through which they had passed.[4] At the July Congress of the Communist International, Hannington used the miners' march to illustrate the need for unemployed workers' movements in all countries, and in this respect to criticise the perspectives offered by Bukharin, the principal Marxist economist and theoretician left in the Soviet Union. Bukharin had delivered the main report of the Executive Committee on the world situation. Hannington was sharply critical, since his report put too little emphasis on the question of unemployment and the unemployed. He felt that 'Neglect of this enormous field ... constitutes a very serious error on the part of the International.' The work was as important as trade union activity, because it, too, could be used to undermine the reformist leaders. The miners' march had been the 'biggest mass activity in Britain since 1927', and if the International persisted in ignoring the unemployed, then 'We are not entitled to say that we are the practical leaders of the masses.' The Communist International should instruct all Communist Parties to set up movements along NUWCM lines. Hannington's speech had certainly been in line with a feeling among the delegates that the unemployment issue had been underestimated by Soviet theoreticians; when the economist Varga was forced to agree that they had indeed failed in this direction, the sober official record reported 'prolonged cheers'. Bukharin himself, remarking on Hannington's speech in his summary reply, said that his intervention had been important, and that 'the most serious attention' would have to be paid to the matter.[5]

These interventions by Horner and Hannington were apposite and astute. They had bowed to the orthodoxy whilst expressing reservations that were in reality heretical. Both men could now be considered significant Communists in an international sense. Not many British Communists conducted a successful exchange with Bukharin, after all. Much more importantly, however, these contributions played a part in turning the attention of Communists all over the world towards the importance of establishing unemployed movements. Some such movements already existed, but their number appears to have increased world-wide in the late 1920s. These organisations were to play an important role (one almost entirely ignored by historians) in the world economic crisis of the early 1930s. The miners' march, then, had unforeseen consequences on an international level.

The 1928 TUC Congress

The TUC Congress held in Swansea in September 1928 showed how the new political line had affected the movement, but it also confirmed the Communist Party and the NUWCM in their conviction that they could successfully fight TUC policies. Soon after his return from the Soviet Union, Hannington led a march of some 2,000 miners from the West Wales coalfield to the Congress. The tone of their demonstrations outside the Congress was very hostile to the TUC. In references to the TUC's discussions with the industrialist Mond, they denounced the delegates as 'Mondite bureaucrats'. The hostility was mutual.

An important debate took place at the Conference, regarding the desirability of the TUC setting up its own unemployed organisation. During the previous year, a limited experiment had been attempted, the results of which strongly influenced the discussion. In 1927, the Bristol Unemployed Association, run on non-NUWCM lines by the local Labour Party, was reorganised to bring it under the Trades Council's control. The committee of the Association was re-formed on the basis of representation from City Councillors, the Board of Guardians, the churches, and the unemployed.[6] At the inaugural meeting,

when Walter Baker, a Labour MP, and the Bishop of Bristol
spoke, the object of the association was said to be to put
pressure on the government to come to the assistance of local
authorities but without taking any political stands.[7] It seems
to have been difficult for the association to keep politics
entirely out of its proceedings, however. At a branch meeting
in early 1928, a motion was proposed that 'work or full
maintenance' should be an aim of the association. In the
spring, the South Wales Organiser of the Young Communist
League was invited to the Central Branch of the association,
and it was reported that a request came from the 200 workless
present for a branch of the NUWCM to be formed.[8] By the
summer of 1928, the NUWCM was definitely increasing its
membership in Bristol.[9] This is essential background to the
TUC discussions, because it appears that the TUC's efforts in
Bristol had been entirely counter-productive.

The NUWCM was refused permission to address the TUC
Conference, but the debate on unemployed associations could
not have gone better for it. The General Council proposed the
formation of associations which would take up relief
questions, organise meetings and arrange social and
educational activities. The object was to be to 'combine in one
organisation employed and unemployed persons for com-
batting evils arising from unemployment'.[10] Davies of the
Miners' Federation moved the reference back. He argued that
it would mean that 'people who are doing nothing else but
trying to rend the unions in twain, will be given an
opportunity to do it.' He could not see what authority there
would be over the associations, and he was supported in this
by Dukes of the General and Municipal Workers. Reference
was made to the NUWCM as the principal adversary.[11] The
reference back was carried. The Communist paper *Workers'
Life* reported their decision on 7 September by saying:

> The unemployed have been deserted by the gang who control
> the TUC. The order had gone out that there is to be no real
> organisation of the workless, even in the emasculated scab
> committees with which the General Council has been playing.

The decision could have been seen as a victory for the
unemployed movement, but the Communist Party still
preferred to use it as a stick with which to beat the TUC, so

bitter were feelings between the two organisations.

The reference back of the General Council's proposal was important for the NUWCM, because it meant that its revival was carried on without substantial opposition from the trade unions at local level. The TUC, had it had the will, could have begun to build its own unemployed organisation in 1928. There were many local unemployed associations outside of the NUWCM, as the Bristol association's success in the early 1920s exemplified. Many within the labour movement saw a need to keep the unemployed away from the Communist Party and from the activities of church and philanthropic middle-class people at local level. Had the TUC not been so concerned about control over any organisations which were set up, it might have been able to build an alternative to the NUWCM.

The Scottish Miners' March and the Canadian Episode

A Conference of Scottish NUWCM branches was held in June 1928. The meeting reflected Hannington's preparatory campaign in the Fife and Lanarkshire coalfields, which had resulted in seven new NUWCM branches being formed.[12] The conference concluded that the Welsh miners' march had been the most important event in the workers' movement during 1927, that the problems in Scotland were similar and that a special committee should be formed to plan a march from the mining areas to Edinburgh to meet the Scottish Board of Health to demand full relief for the large numbers of workless pitmen.[13] Just at this time, as the march was being decided upon, unemployed miners were faced with a further problem. The Ministry of Labour began that summer to 'invite' men in the mining areas to travel to Canada to work gathering in the harvest. Refusal could be taken to mean that people were 'Not Genuinely Seeking Work' and had therefore forfeited their right to benefit. The NUWCM was strongest in the mining areas, and organised locally to deal with the resulting problems. Many grievances of the miners who went to Canada were raised by the Scottish marchers, but the movement also organised amongst those who went.

The late summer of 1928 saw a 'lightning campaign' to recruit 10,000 men, most of them miners and all of them unmarried, to go to Canada for the harvest. All kinds of promises were made about what they would find on the other side of the Atlantic. Men were shipped over in cramped quarters in ships, and then simply sent off to try to find work either harvesting or in the coalfield, in competition with Poles and Southern Europeans. Wage rates of two dollars a day were commonly paid, which meant that many men would be unable to pay their fare back to Britain. Travelling back to Winnipeg, hundreds of men were interned in an underground cage with an armed guard at the door. The story is continued by Patrick Keogh, a miner:

> Feeling ran high when the immigration authorities, after three days, demanded we should take a job at no guaranteed wages or starve. There was an uproar, and when the men became hungry, cafes were looted. A policeman got hold of one of our pals, and when an attempt was made to rescue him, the policeman drew a revolver ... he was sent to jail for two months. There were plenty of Canadian harvesters seeking work, and they resented our intrusion – we were hissed when we landed.[14]

On the ships going over, and in the immigration halls, unemployed men from the NUWCM were active, along with Canadian trade unionists. By the middle of September, ships were returning. On one of these was T. Tierney, who explained that they had forced the Canadian Pacific to ship them back to Britain free of charge.[15] On another was a group who refused to speak except through their elected shipboard committee, one of whose members said that he had been better off as a prisoner of war than he had been in Canada. One man told the press that they had written their story, but if the press wanted it they would have to pay for it. Another was threatened with violence when he gave reporters a leaflet which had been given out saying:

> Comrades, we have been the victims of a huge conspiracy of international capitalism to get rid of us in Britain, a conspiracy that has been entered into by the Tory government of Great Britain and the Liberal Government of Canada. We are only the first contingent in a great scheme to rid British capitalism of its own contradictory evils.[16]

But if there had clearly been effective agitation among the miners, there had also been fertile ground for it, as John Townsend of Barrow explained:

> It has been suggested that the whole thing was a 'Red' agitation
> against the government, but it was nothing of the kind. Politics
> did not worry us, and the only agitation was by men who had
> been badly deceived and were restless at the deception.[17]

The activity amongst those who went to Canada had been in
some ways successful, in that it brought many men home free of
charge, and at the same time created a considerable furore in
Britain which forced the Canadian Minister of Labour to admit
that exploitative wages had been offered to many. He must have
persuaded at least some unemployed that emigration was not
an effective answer to their problems.[18]

Some of the returning harvesters arrived in Scotland in time
for the march. About 250 men marched from Lanarkshire,
Stirlingshire and Fifeshire, led by Hannington. The men
attracted support from many people along the route. The
Scottish Co-op provided food, and a separate women's
contingent organised by the Edinburgh Trades Council met
the marchers at the edge of the town and escorted them in.
Perhaps the most interesting feature of the march was the way
that marchers were treated as delegates by the unemployed
from their areas, who asked for grievances to be raised in
Edinburgh. As a result, the Board of Health had some 200 cases
of parish council treatment put before it, and agreed to consider
any further cases provided that they were forwarded through
the NUWCM. It also agreed that the NUWCM had a right to
represent claimants at the Courts of Referees which
adjudicated on appeals over insurance benefits. Here was an
important amount of recognition by the state, which dealt a
blow to the idea held by the majority of parish councillors in
Scotland that the unemployed had no rights and could only
expect charity. Mention of the NUWCM as the organisation
through which problems should be channelled was almost
equally important. The Board of Health clearly wanted a
channel through which it could discuss the problems raised,
but for the NUWCM this decision was equivalent to a
recommendation from the Scottish Board of Health to join the
unemployed movement if people wanted to go beyond their
parish councils. These were important principles, conceded for
the first time. If that were not enough, the marchers also
extracted an agreement from the Ministry of Labour officials

present that people who had gone to Canada as harvesters would be entitled to benefit again on their return. It is hardly surprising, then, to see the Communist paper *Workers' Life* greeting these agreements with the triumphant headline: 'Recognition Won From Board of Health and Ministry of Labour For Unemployed Committees'.[19]

The Second National Hunger March

The Scottish march had not only brought great gains in terms of recognition, it had even resulted in a financial surplus, which it was decided to carry over for a National Hunger March, the first to take place since 1922-23. Nearly 1,000 men marched from all over Britain to protest at the Not Genuinely Seeking Work clause and the 30 stamp requirement. Only two of the leaders of the 1922 march also led the second march: Hannington and Sid Elias, who had learned a good deal from their earlier experience. Elias, who had been District Secretary for Wales and a NAC member in the early 1920s, was asked to join Hannington as a paid organiser for the movement. An able speaker, organiser and Communist, he made a large contribution over the next seven years. Jointly with Hannington, he made the 1929 march a considerable success. From the standpoint of its internal organisation, 1929 represented a notable step forward. Marchers were very carefully selected by local committees, and given more detailed instructions on what they were to bring, and what to expect. A regular *March Circular* was sent out by NUWCM headquarters to all committees, and Marchers' Defence Councils set up in areas from which the marchers came to look after their families and to publicise the march locally. In this way, it was ensured that it would not only be the localities through which the contingents passed that were to be in action.[20] The march was quite successful. The policy of the Ministry of Health, which was to try to encourage local workhouse officers to treat the men as 'casuals' (that is, vagrants) and to give them the very poor food and accommodation that 'casuals' received, was substantially broken. Contingents were able to put sufficient pressure on local officials to persuade them to ignore this advice. In the end, the government also had to beat a retreat. The 30 stamp requirement was withdrawn for twelve months, just three days after the end of the march.[21]

The march had met with varied receptions from local labour movement bodies; life had in this sense been a little more difficult for them than it had been for the Welsh miners. Trades Councils on the route had been circularised by the TUC telling them in no uncertain terms that it did not support the venture. The unemployed movement was therefore faced with a new difficulty: that of justifying itself and its activities to a labour movement encouraged to see the NUWCM as being outside of its ranks.

It is interesting, therefore, to look at the nature of the discussions on one Trades Council along the route of the Scottish contingent. The Northampton Trades Council was in particularly close touch with the TUC, and the majority of delegates generally argued in favour of the TUC's attitude to the NUWCM. In September 1928, sharp exchanges took place at the Trades Council over the NUWCM's march to the Swansea TUC. The unemployed movement was attacked for organising the demonstration for its own benefit, and exploiting the workless 'for the purpose of a set-off against the official trade union movement' as one critic put it.[22] Attewell, a prominent left-winger, replied that the real disrupters were union officials, who expelled activists for their opinions. The left was then told that it was the task of the unions to organise the workless, but replied that the unions had had no success in this and that if its opponents were interested, then 'You try it on'.[23] Undeterred, the movement's critics said that marches to the TUC 'only added to the distress of the unemployed and did them no good at all'.[24] The left accused the Swansea Co-op of refusing the marchers food, to which the right replied that they had no money. Criticism of the TUC was wrong, the right went on, because the TUC was sincere in wanting to help the unemployed; sincerity was not demonstrated, though, by organising useless marches.[25]

The prospect of the Hunger Marchers coming through Northampton, and the fact that the march was directed against the government and not the TUC, changed the terms of the debate in the movement's favour. On 16 January 1929, the Council met in committee to consider a formal request from Harry McShane on behalf of the march organising committee, for two meals and accommodation when it arrived on 17 February. This was formally proposed, but a wrecking 'amendment' was put arguing that because of distress in Northampton and because the time was 'inopportune', the organising committee should be told that nothing could be provided and the march should not come through the town. The NUWCM's supporters argued that the Council had a responsibility to the marchers, and scored a notable victory by defeating the amendment by fifteen votes to eleven.[25] The Trades Council executive then began a campaign to nullify this vote. First it passed a resolution asking the organising committee for an assurance that nothing 'injurious' to the labour movement would be said at any public meeting in the town, and then invited a Mrs Simpson of the Board of Guardians to inform Council delegates of the problems of accommodating the marchers in the workhouse. At the meeting at which she spoke, a motion was proposed, 'That in view of the large amount of unemployment and short-time working, also the fact that the march is being organised by a body not recognised by either the TUC or Labour Party, the application be not entertained'. The motion was defeated.[27] Four days before the contingent was due to arrive, accommodation had been secured at the YMCA, and the Co-op had agreed to provide each man with a food parcel. Once the column had arrived, the earlier wrangling disappeared and many Trades Council delegates came to help 150 footsore marchers who, it was reported to the Council's next meeting, 'conducted themselves as gentlemen'.[28] This was the only occasion between the wars that the Northampton Trades Council supported a Hunger March. In general, the delegates accepted the arguments that the marches were not official and did the unemployed no practical good. In 1929, exceptionally, these arguments were successfully confronted by the left.

Hannington was well aware of the kinds of arguments that had gone on locally, and realised that the movement was at a crucial point in its relationship with the wider labour movement. All of the basic arguments about the need for a separate organisation of unemployed, and the importance of Hunger Marches needed to be rehearsed to a wide audience. He therefore wrote his longest report on a march, a 71 page booklet *The Story of the National Hunger March*. Sold at threepence, it was published only about a month after the end of the events it described. After explaining the specific reasons for the march, Hannington addressed the TUC's contention that unnecessary hardship had been inflicted on those taking part. His replies were that all the men who had participated had been made fully aware of what lay before them both through the recruiting leaflet and in personal interviews, and that personal hardship was preferable to the torture of watching one's family sink into despair and even starve. Here was the essential spirit of the unemployed movement: that, by fighting, the workless retained their self-respect and dignity as human beings. As Hannington pointed out, it was hoped that by refusing to remain silent in their misery, the unemployed would raise public awareness of their situation and improvements would be won. But concrete steps forward were not guaranteed, and were not the only justification. It was actually the case that the march had brought an improvement: the suspension of the 30-stamp rule. To regard this as the only argument for action was however quite wrong in Hannington's view. The important point for the unemployed was to assert themselves.[29]

The Hunger March had certainly stimulated many unemployed to follow Hannington's advice and to join the NUWCM. The marchers were asked to return to their homes and to organise recruiting drives. New branches were being set up, whilst existing ones recruited hundreds of new members. A new branch was formed in Liverpool just after the end of the march, the Bristol branch had become 'very strong', and a committee was reformed in Coventry. The NUWCM was reviving in the main towns.[30] But during the spring of 1929, Hannington was nominated by the Communist Party to fight Wallsend against his arch-enemy Margaret Bondfield, in the General Election. The CPGB's choice of Hannington to contest Bondfield's seat was made so that the Communists could 'expose' Bondfield, as it hoped to expose all reformists. The campaign was more than lively, with Hannington vigorously attacking his opponents with the help of a small band of Communist Party and NUWCM stalwarts. In return, he received considerable abuse from the local press, being described by the *North Mail* as 'the notorious Wal Hannington, who was largely responsible for duping unemployed miners into "hunger marches".[31] Margaret Bondfield was able to carry on her campaign without engaging in any real debate about her role on the Blanesburgh Committee, yet this did not create any difficulties for her on polling day. She was elected with a majority of 7,105, whilst Hannington came bottom of the poll with 744 votes.[32] The election showed that whilst some of the unemployed could be persuaded to protest with the unemployed movement, the majority of their number would not vote for a Communist in preference to the Labour Party. Hannington might have been better deployed continuing to build up the NUWCM.

The Communist Party's leadership was not pleased with Hannington's politics at this point. He was considered insufficiently zealous in attacking the reformists, and too jealous of the NUWCM's independence. Whilst Pollitt insistently pursued the new Communist line of strong hostility to reformist leaders, Hannington harboured reservations. The precise nature and extent of these arguments remains unclear despite some public disagreements between the two men around this time, and this led to their estrangement for the rest of their lives.[33] Certainly, the party leadership as a whole was not enamoured of Hannington: at the 1929 Communist Party Congress he was not recommended for re-election to the Central Committee, but the Congress delegates recognised Hannington as a leader of genuine mass struggles, and elected him regardless.[34] The recent marches had confirmed his reputation with the CPGB's membership, if not with the party leadership.

The Second Labour Government

The 1929 General Election brought the Labour Party into government with the support of the Liberals. The NUWCM leaders regarded the government with a very critical eye. This was not only because of the new policies reigning within the CPGB. The Cabinet was not as apparently 'left' as its 1924 predecessor. Wheatley had been excluded, and Lansbury relegated to the Office of Works. Snowden, at the Treasury, was an advocate of reduced public spending, and soon made it plain that expenditure on public works schemes would be relatively small, rendering its impact negligible. Nor had the Labour Party's programme appealed to the NUWCM. Emigration had been advocated for the first time, whilst the party had been outflanked by the Liberals on the unemployment issue. Yet there were also some hopeful signs, such as the removal of the hated Commissioners who had replaced the Guardians at West

Ham, Chester-le-Street and Bedwellty.

The new government did not induce a decline in the
unemployed movement's membership and activity as the
election of the 1924 government had. Unemployment
continued to rise during 1929, and some of the uncritical
optimism of 1924 was dispelled by the Communist Party's new
line. In fact, the NUWCM was able to launch a major
mobilisation in the summer of 1929. In July, there were
demonstrations in most major towns, which was an
achievement in itself in view of the general tendency for
agitation to slump during the summer months. Much of this
mobilisation was directed against the Not Genuinely Seeking
Work clause, which had been at the centre of the movement's
work for some time already. Bas Barker of the Chesterfield
branch, then a young Communist engineer, recalled the
situation locally, linking it explicitly with the position in 1986:

> They did a 'Restart' programme then. You had to prove
> yourself to be genuinely seeking employment, and you had a
> green card, and you were supposed to take this green card to the
> Exchange to tell them where you'd been to inquire for a job.
> Well, obviously, it were a nonsense, I mean, well, bloody hell,
> I'm going down to Donkins [a local engineering works, RC]
> etc., and so on ... 'take your bloody hook'. You know what they'd
> say. So we had got to try and do something to break this rule and
> we practised this here and in Sheffield, and we organised *mass*
> applications. About two or three hundred people to march
> down to Donkins, and they'd sign green card, see. And other
> firms, Markham [a local pit, RC], these firms ... so they played
> bloody hell with the Labour Exchange, and they dropped it.
> They said, 'Oh, well, don't bloody bother,' you know, because
> obviously the firms were saying, 'What do you want us to do, set
> a bleeding clerk on to sign a bloke's green card to say he's been
> and applied for a job?' And that broke that.[35]

Similar actions were carried out all over Britain, with the effect
that by the autumn of 1929 the system had become largely
inoperable. The clause was considerably diluted when
parliament returned from the summer recess.

Another attempt to organise the workless failed completely,
and this was a projected campaign against 'transference'. The
scheme was an important part of the official response to
unemployment, and involved helping people who wanted to
move away from the 'depressed areas' of the North to the South

and employment. Hannington roundly denounced the scheme as it worked in practice, and focused on one particular case to make his point. He publicised how John Devine, a Lanarkshire miner, was sent to the Kent coalfield, and, unable to tolerate the high underground temperatures and 'driving' by the supervision, had come to the NUWCM offices in London for help. Hannington decided to fight his case on the basis that the Labour Exchange should either find Devine a job, or give him his fare home. Devine returned to the Kent coalfield with Sid Elias to try to begin a campaign against the transference scheme. The intention was to organise people in the same plight to make up a deputation to the Ministry of Labour. This proved impossible, because although there were many miners in Kent who were discontented with the scheme, these men were constantly on the move between jobs, and many were returning home. Devine himself, according to Hannington, was 'very much dejected' by his experience, and tried to walk home. He died of hunger and exhaustion on the road, an unsung fighter, one of the unemployed movement's martyrs, recorded in death by officialdom as a 'vagrant'.[36] The proposed campaign expired with him. This was one of many abortive initiatives launched by the leaders of the NUWCM. In this particular case, the problem had lain in the fact that the unemployed men were scattered, away from home and on the move. It was a negative demonstration of the relevance of the relative immobility of the majority of the unemployed to the existence of the NUWCM. It also showed the way in which the movement was always looking for new ways of organising, undeterred by the disappointment which frequently followed.

The failure of the campaign against transference encouraged the Labour government and its successors to pursue the idea of moving the unemployed from 'depressed areas' to the South and Midlands with increasing vigour. This had the political advantage for governments of portraying unemployment as a regional rather than a national problem. The unemployed movement tried to take this advantage away by arguing that work should be found people where they were. At a more practical level, they also tried to dissuade the workless from uprooting themselves. Rather than organise the transferees, they turned towards stopping people from moving away in the first place.

The Sixth National Conference, 1929

The Sixth National Conference brought 82 delegates together. The atmosphere was very much one of defiant Communism. In the words of the Conference report, 'The hall had been decorated with banners and slogans of the movement, and the colour was red.'[37] There were none of the fierce and disorderly debates of earlier Conferences, when there had been more passion and less concern for the rules of debate. All of the principal resolutions were proposed by headquarters, and passed.

The Conference agreed to change the name of the movement, dropping 'Committee' from its title, to make it 'National Unemployed Workers' Movement' (NUWM). The change of name was in one sense useful, in that it shortened it and therefore made it clearer to the non-member. However, the new title can also be seen as a recognition that the committees which had played such an important part in the early years of the movement's history, had now become much less important in relation to the national headquarters. In this sense, it was a straw in the wind.

Whilst Hannington and Arthur Horner opened the Conference by expounding Communist theories on unemployment, and criticising the Labour Party, the most important and lasting decisions concerned the NUWM's internal organisation. Conference adopted a set of rules and a Constitution. The rules were revealing. Branches were required to read and discuss headquarters circulars, and the headquarters committee was further strengthened. Renamed the 'Headquarters Advisory Committee', it was to consist of 'capable comrades residing in the London area', selected by the NAC.[38] In other words, it was not to be elected from Conference, as had previously been the case. It was to meet weekly at headquarters, and in practice became the day-to-day governing body of the NUWM, the expression of the paid officials' authority.

The Conference ratified decisions which had initially come from a meeting at headquarters held at the end of 1928. These decisions concerned the establishment of legal and women's departments. The legal department was considered necessary because of the greatly increased volume and importance of claims to the National Insurance Umpire, and was to be financed by a levy on branches. The law surrounding benefit had become increasingly complex, and the local 'penny lawyers' who existed within the movement at local level needed expert advice. Sid Elias was the first person to staff this department, and studied assiduously to acquire both expertise and a national library on legal matters. The women's department was set up on the initiative of Mrs Youle, a Labour Party delegate from the only women's section present, Sheffield, who was one of the few with any practical experience of organising unwaged women. The department was charged with improving women's involvement at local level. At the NAC meeting held immediately after the Conference, Maud Brown became head of the new department. Her appointment marked the beginning of a rapid and qualitative improvement in the movement's work among women. Like Lillian Thring before her, Brown was a non-CPGB middle-class radical of great energy. It is interesting to note that Brown and Thring showed social origins and political allegiances different to those of the working-class male leadership of the NUWM. Confident, assertive women, they were able to make their mark in a milieu which women of more proletarian origins seem to have found more dificult. Accepting neither pay nor expenses, she became a national leader of the NUWM, and was to help change the movement's nature and image in the 1930s.[39]

A decision was also taken which was designed to strengthen links with employed workers in the period of TUC hostility. The NUWM was 'withholding' its demand for affiliation to the TUC, and therefore decided to encourage the employed to join the NUWM. Employed people were to be admitted to committees, provided that they did not make up more than one-third of that body's number.[40] The Conference also agreed to build a 'joint working relationship' with the Minority Movement. This was in line with the general policy of unifying the employed and unemployed, but in practice it did not mean a great deal. By this time the MM was a rump organisation, and the decision meant little more than one to forge a partnership with employed Communists. The main result was that the NUWM was very soon to be the MM's dominant section.[41]

The 1929 Conference had in many respects been a rather routine affair enlivened mainly by rousing statements of Communist militancy and solidarity rather than profound discussion. There was no serious debate of any dimensions recounted in the Conference *Report*. The hegemony of the group of Communist officials around the prestigious Hannington was more apparent than ever. Although there were still non-Communists in the NAC like Len Youle of Sheffield, they were very much 'fellow-travellers' who never mounted any opposition to the main strategic decisions. Yet the dominance of Communists was not yet the dominance of CPGB headquarters. The NUWM's leadership quietly maintained its independence without being too explicit. Whilst this attitude did not go unnoticed, there was little that Communist Party leaders could do in practice to subordinate the NUWM more comprehensively without destroying its appeal to the unemployed as a whole. The NUWM might not spend sufficient time and energy attacking 'reformists', but it was recognised that its main function was to represent the unemployed and not to lead political campaigns.

Within the unemployed movement, headquarters ran affairs to a much greater extent than it had in the early 1920s. Circular after circular rained down on branches: the rule of 'Comrade Gestetner' had begun. But this rule was not just sterile bureaucracy; it was rather an attempt to bring order and co-ordination to an already volcanic series of local eruptions. Revolt was very much in the air and demonstrations, meetings and marches were breaking out all over the country. The Wall Street crash was just six weeks away, and mass activity had already begun. The NUWM was poised to lead the unemployed into their greatest struggles yet.

Notes

1 236 of the 654 members were in arrears in March 1927, but this represented an improvement on the proportion in arrears in June 1926, which was approximately 50 per cent on the only page of the contributions book recording arrears. Mardy NUWCM, Register of Members' Contributions, December 1925-June 1927. (Mardy Lodge, F, South Wales Coalfield Archive.)
2 Francis and Smith, op.cit., p.101.
3 *Workers' Life*, 6 May 1927.
4 Red International of Labour Unions, *Protokoll des IV Kongresses der RGI, 1928*, Berlin 1928, pp.191-3, 569.
5 *Inprecorr*, Vol.8, No.44, pp.89-91; Vol.8, No.46, pp.817-9; *Report* of the

Sixth World Congress of the Communist International, sixteenth session, 30 July 1928.

6 Whitfield, op.cit., pp.221-8.
7 *Western Daily Press*, 30 September 1927.
8 *Workers' Weekly*, 13 January, 23 March 1928.
9 Whitfield, op.cit., pp.320-3.
10 TUC Congress *Report* 1928, pp.111-3.
11 Ibid., pp.311-2.
12 *Workers' Life*, 7 September 1928.
13 W. Hannington, *Our March Against the Starvation Government*, London 1928, p.5; *Workers' Life*, 22 June 1928.
14 *Catholic Herald*, 22 September 1928.
15 *Forward* (Glasgow), 29 September 1928.
16 *Liverpool Post and Mercury*, 15 September 1928.
17 *Barrow Guardian*, 22 September 1928.
18 *Catholic Herald*, 29 September 1928.
19 *Workers' Life*, 28 September 1928.
20 *March Circular*, nos 7 and 12 (Cumbria Record Office, BDX/93).
21 Kingsford, op.cit., p.108.
22 Unidentified newspaper cutting, 20 September 1928, in *Minutes* of the Northampton Trades Council (Northants Record Office).
23 Ibid.
24 Ibid.
25 Ibid.
26 *Minutes* of the Northampton Trades Council, 16 Janaury 1929.
27 Ibid., 31 January 1929.
28 Ibid., 13 February, 20 March 1929.
29 W. Hannington, *The Story of the National Hunger March*, London 1929, pp.4-5, 69-71.
30 *Workers' Life*, 5 April 1929; *Minutes* of the Coventry branch of the Minority Movement, 19 December 1929, (Modern Records Centre, University of Warwick).
31 *North Mail*, 12 April 1929.
32 J.M. Bellamy and J. Saville (eds), *Dictionary of Labour Biography*, Vol.2 London 1974, pp.42-3.
33 Interview with Winnie Hannington by Doug Low (date unknown).
34 Kingsford, op.cit., p.113.
35 Interview with Bas Barker, 6 August 1986.
36 *Workers' Life*, 7 June 1929.
37 *Report* of the Sixth National Conference, p.1.
38 Ibid., p.4.
39 S. Bruley, 'Socialism and Feminism in the Communist Party of Great Britain, 1920-1939', unpublished PhD Thesis, London School of Economics, 1980, pp.243-4.
40 *Report* of the Sixth National Conference, p.6, 11-3.
41 Ibid.

6

The Crash, the Means Test and Starvation, 1930-33

The World Slump

The 1930s saw the world economic system in a crisis from which it only fully emerged during the Second World War. Whilst the 1920s had brought what could be called a 'home-grown' depression in Britain, the following decade was one of profound international slump. The consequences in Britain were milder than in the USA and Germany. World trade fell by about one-third from its 1929 level. The worse years were the first four; reflationary policies in the USA and Germany led recovery after 1933 and dispelled the worst features of the slump.

The economic crisis had an immediate and shocking material consequence for the working class: the onset of mass unemployment on an unprecedented scale. Throughout the industrialised world workers were thrown out of employment with neither notice nor compensation. During 1930, the average number registered as unemployed in Britain shot up to 1,917,000; the following year brought an increase, whilst 1932 registered 2,745,000. Gradual economic recovery began in 1933 with an improvement in the volume of goods produced; the pool of registered workless gradually contracted as the decade continued, but still remained at over 1,500,000 in 1939.[1] The crisis of the early 1930s was in many respects more serious for the unemployed than that of the 1980s has been: the rate of unemployment was higher, because the national workforce was considerably smaller; there were no redundancy payments and low wages allowed very little savings; benefit levels meant that the drop in living standards was very much more serious than it is today. The workless had their backs to the wall in a sense that it is hard to grasp some fifty years later.

Unemployment in Britain was still centred, as it had been in the 1920s, on the staple manufacturing and extractive industries of the North, Scotland and Wales. But unemployment became a more national phenomenon in the 1930s, with the Midlands and South registering higher numbers out of work than previously. At the same time, successive governments intensified their efforts to treat the problem as essentially regional, through transference and regional aid policies. It was clearly not in their interests to encourage a perception of unemployment as a national issue. Unemployment also cast its shadow over previously sheltered social strata. By the beginning of the 1930-31 school year, the *Manchester Guardian* was carrying articles about out-of-work school teachers.[2] This was a particular threat to white-collar women: by 1936, the same paper was canvassing 'solutions' to the teachers' difficulties which involved reductions in the already small number of married women teachers at work.[3] There were now whole strata of white-collar workers who saw that the possibility of being pushed out of work was not limited to manual workers. Since there were larger concentrations of such workers in the South, this also encouraged them to recognise that, although the government might speak of 'distressed areas', these were part of a distressed country.

As the NUWM had always stressed, the tribulations of the workless had important effects in the employed working class. Despite the rising real wages of the time, the 1930s were a decade of consuming dread of the sack. Workers were reminded of their dependence on wages both for the necessities of life and for the right to assert their personal independence as citizens and adults. There were many managers prepared to play on their fears, who had no scruples about conjuring up the image of a desperate 'reserve army' waiting at the factory gates for the jobs of those who expressed dissatisfaction with their wages or conditions. The employed knew only too well the absolute poverty, deprivation and humiliation which came with being out of work; many in their own communities and families were living reminders of these realities. It is little wonder that for many older people the 1930s were a decisive experience, a decade to which they have no wish to return in even an approximate way.

The majority of the workforce remained in work during the 1930s, of course, and for members of the NUWM, it was felt to be essential to draw this majority of employed workers, with their economic and political power, into the struggles of the unemployed if real gains were to be made. The problem, however, was that the gap between those in and out of work was widening during the 1930s. The standard of living for those in employment actually improved. Taking 1924 as the base year, and weekly real wages in that year as 100, wages in the worst year of the slump, 1932, stood at 116.5. They never fell below 113.5 for the rest of the decade, largely because of falling prices.[4] Meanwhile, cuts in benefit in 1932 of 10 per cent (later restored), the impact of the Family Means Test which looked at the resources available to each family before allowing any individual benefit and tighter control over trade union unemployment benefits almost certainly brought declining standards of living for the majority of the unemployed, until 1935. The state of industrial relations worked in the same direction. Trade unionists saw little point in attempting strike action in the first half of the decade. Working days lost through strikes therefore remained lower than they had been for much of the 1920s. This meant in turn that there was less opportunity for the NUWM to build strong links with those taking strike action as it had done in the early 1920s. There was a weakening of the relations with active trade unionists more generally because of this, which made it increasingly difficult to look for contributions from local union branches to NUWM funds. Still less was it the case, at least in the first half of the decade, that the traditional demand of the NUWM, that employed workers should take action in favour of the unemployed, could be fulfilled. There were only limited and localised examples of this as employment began to pick up, and, in general, the workless struggled in isolation. This gulf between those in and out of work was a major limiting factor in the potential gains which could be made by the agitations of the unemployed, however extensive and impressive they might have been. Governments could always reflect that, however much active discontent there was among the workless, there was little possibility of this discontent being mirrored amongst the employed. The 'unity of the employed and unemployed' so often called for by the leaders of the NUWM remained a rhetorical device rather than a reality.

The NUWM in 1930

For the Communists who led the unemployed movement in 1930, it appeared that the final capitalist crisis had arrived. Crises were part and parcel of the anarchic pattern of capitalist development, and the unemployed were the principal victims, displaced from the workforce as the capitalist class sought to restructure its system to raise the rate of profit. Contrasting the situation of the world capitalist order with what they saw as the beginnings of a planned economy in the Soviet Union, many Communists found ample justification for their activity in the comparison. Here was the death agony of an outmoded and oppressive system. Here, too, was an opportunity for Communists to seize the leadership of the labour movement. If the Communist Party pursued a clear enough line, then workers would flock to their banner, deserting the TUC and Labour Party. In 1930, the long awaited Communist daily paper, the *Daily Worker*, was launched, the weapon with which it was hoped to smash the opposition.

These views seemed to them in many ways borne out by the nature of the NUWM in 1930. The movement's organisational state gradually improved. Membership had stood at about 10,000 in 1929, but by July 1930 it was reported that contribution stamp purchases (a reliable indicator of the number of real members) had reached 39,000.[5] The type of member coming into the movement also gave cause for hope. They were younger and tended to be 'newer and less demoralised' as an NAC *Report* put it.[6] They were more likely to want to take action than some of their predecessors, who had been more ground down by their experiences. Moreover, many of them were not labour movement activists with qualms about taking measures which might embarrass the Labour government. The Minority Movement's paper the *Worker* noted this new type of member with approval, and said

that it had already led to the NUWM becoming more
organised around collective action, and less around 'case-
fighting'.[7] Many of those who wore the new NUWM badge of
1930 ('NUWM' in black on a red background) were soon
drawn into action. This membership combined with 'Third
Period' Communist politics to lead the South Walian
Communist Lewis Jones to argue vigorously that the
NUWM should 'transform itself' from being a trade union for
the unemployed, into a 'revolutionary organisation'.[8] Jones
seems to have felt, like others before him, that the unemployed
could be at the forefront of revolutionary activity.
Hannington, on the other hand, was always quick to point out
the limitations of the unemployed movement. It was easy to be
carried away by the volcanic eruptions of the unemployed, he
often said, but the unemployed remained a minority within
the working class, without economic power. Whilst constantly
calling on the unemployed to defend themselves, Hannington
remained aware of the inherent limitations of any unemployed
movement.

The arguments of those who would have the NUWM
'transformed' into a revolutionary organisation took little
account of the problems which the movement still had despite
its revival. The small number of people involved in running
branches, the ephemeral nature of many branches (especially
the smaller ones), the general shortage of finance and the lack
of a national newspaper constituted a network of quite serious
difficulties. But, in this period of Communist history, there
were many who were inclined to press on in the
'revolutionary' direction and to blame the rank and file when
results were poor. Even Hannington was drawn into this type
of attitude. On 6 March, the Communist International called
an 'International Day of Struggle' against unemployment.
Demonstrations were to be held all over the industrialised
world. This was something of a flop in Britain, with only the
faithful turning out. Hannington argued that this was due to
lack of adequate preparation, but the lack of specific demands
must have rendered it only partially relevant to the
unemployed.

The Seventh National Conference, held in Bradford in
February 1931, heard that the failure of the International Day
of Struggle was the result of a 'failure to carry out correct mass

work'. The failure of the NUWM was contrasted with the continual development of 'mass activity' in Germany and the USA.[9] Hannington similarly criticised the work of the movement in the woollen industry lock-out of 1930, during which the NUWM was very active in trying to obtain relief for the locked-out workers. The problem, Hannington argued, was that the leading NUWM members were so immersed in the work of the strike committee 'that many weaknesses were discernible, particularly the absence of a distinct campaign among the unemployed'.[10] These criticisms were typical of the Communist Party in this period, and concealed serious underlying problems within the party's politics. The woollen lock-out, referred to inaccurately by the CPGB at the time as 'the woollen strike', was not a dispute with the revolutionary potential ascribed to it by the sloganising *Daily Worker*. The 'many weaknesses' to which Hannington referred stemmed primarily from the tendency to encourage NUWM activists to think that it had a far more hopeful prospect of changing society than it actually had. A more realistic assessment might have helped militants not to become too embroiled in the strike committee. This hyper-critical attitude to the exhausted activists could only have the damaging result of demoralising people. It was little wonder, then, that in the Communist Party itself, membership fell dramatically, so that only a miserable 2,550 were paying dues by the end of 1930.[11] Paradoxically, it was the NUWM that saved the party from total isolation. Whilst Communists redoubled their party work, thinking of themselves as an elite rather than a rump, they desperately needed the NUWM as an organisation with some mass base to bring them out of themselves. Yet this elitist conception of the Communist Party's relationship to the NUWM, and in particular the 'new member', put some limits on the usefulness of the NUWM to the party as a means of rebuilding its strength. Phil Abrahams, a South Walian Communist, recalled:

> We had an opinion in those days that the Communist Party was the vanguard of the workers. You had to be honest, sober, industrious, a good citizen: these were the qualities we were looking for, and of course everybody doesn't come into that.[12]

Mass recruitment was clearly not the order of the day

throughout the Communist Party.

When agitations were in line with the immediate problems of the workless, and used tried and tested methods, the NUWM was still quite successful, as the 1930 Hunger March showed. This march was, as Hannington recognised, 'the biggest test of its kind that the NUWM had ever undertaken. It was an intense and bitter struggle for every group of marchers.'[13] Because the NUWM was isolated from the rest of the labour movement, the march was small with just three hundred and fifty, and was forced into almost total reliance on the poor law institutions for accommodation. There was also the additional, if in a larger sense welcome, problem that the Labour government decided to abolish the Not Genuinely Seeking Work clause just before the march. The 1930 march, although it did not bring any further concessions from the government, did make an important step forward in that a women's contingent took part for the first time. It was a small group. Eight women from Barnsley joined with fourteen in Bradford, and set off for Leeds with Maud Brown at their head. Refusing to be searched or to give up their belongings at Wakefield, they stayed out all night at Sheffield after refusing 'casual' treatment there. The women travelled by coach to Luton, and marched via St Albans to London, arriving on May Day.[14] They were met by a London Women's Committee of Action set up to make arrangements for them, and each woman was presented with a red scarf.[15] Their participation certainly helped to encourage women to participate in the unemployed movement and the marchers, fired with enthusiasm, returned to their areas to campaign.

Co-ordinated campaigns to put pressure on the Public Assistance Committees (PACs) all over the country, were also conducted in 1930. A very extensive agitation for extra relief at Christmas was carried out by the branches in December, a campaign which Hannington noted was 'a considerable advance on previous years'. Such campaigns, behind common demands, allowed opposition to be gradually broken down. Sympathetic PACs made concessions, whereupon others were able to make comparisons to help their case. As the process continued, so more and more forces became available on a regional basis to put pressure on those PACs holding out. This was a theoretical model, but it certainly had a good deal of practical success in the campaign for extra Christmas, and then, when that was largely won, extra winter relief.[16]

The Expansion of Representational Work

It was during 1930 that the NUWM's national Legal Department began to function effectively. The building of an effective information and representation service for individuals whose cases could not be dealt with at branch level was begun after the 1929 Hunger March by Sid Elias, and was carried on by the quiet Glaswegian Jimmy Connolly when Elias went to Moscow. Branches had always spent some time dealing with individual cases, but as the system became more developed and legalistic, so the need for a national response by the NUWM became apparent. The system developed by the unemployed movement worked in the following way: if a member had a problem, he or she approached the branch complaints committee, who provided the person with a representative. It was always stressed by headquarters that it was important for more than one person to know how the procedures worked and that classes needed to be held to teach people how to represent others, so that what it called the 'one-man-band' difficulty could be avoided. This problem was epitomised by the position of 'Fatty' Barraclough, the skilled engineer in Barnsley who had an encyclopaedic knowledge and dealt with almost all local cases. The individual's problem was then taken up with the local official or committee. In the case of any appeal from their decision to the National Insurance Umpire at Kew, the claimant had to be a member of a trade union or the NUWM. The movement therefore had the same rights as trade unions in this matter. Elias and Hannington had claimed these as an organisation representing both unemployed *and* employed people; in 1930, they successfully defended their case to the Umpire, who informed local insurance officials in a famous circular (5809/30). The NUWM's rule book therefore reminded members that a clear contribution card protected their right of appeal.[17] When appeals went to the Umpire, they were normally taken by the branch with the advice and support of the Legal Department; only in a few cases where the problems were especially difficult or important did Head Office send someone to attend. Branches were then supposed to report to the Legal Department on the discussions and decision, although the leadership frequently complained that this was overlooked too often.[18]

The NUWM's legal work expanded enormously during the early 1930s as unemployment increased rapidly and legislation became more complex. Branch complaints committees became very important bodies locally, and many individuals spent virtually their whole time dealing with individual cases. The Legal Department, financed by a levy on branches, began issuing a detailed legal bulletin in 1932. There was no doubt that the NUWM, because it was an organisation which specialised in dealing with these matters, was more effective than trade unions in processing cases. The published results of appeals to the National Insurance Umpire showed this. Over one-third of the total number of cases brought to the Umpire were supported by the NUWM. In 1932, the NUWM brought nearly half of the total.[19] The percentage of disallowances in cases supported by the NUWM was approximately half of the average.[20] The benefits of NUWM representation, then, were very real for the unemployed. This expertise came to be recognised in some trade union branches. The Blackburn branch of the Amalgamated Society of Woodworkers, for example, asked the NUWM to take up all benefit cases for its out-of-work members in 1930.[21] Not all branches were as enthusiastic about the NUWM, but it is interesting to note that, despite the movement's rather tenuous claim to represent both employed and unemployed, no major campaign was initiated by the trade unions to remove the NUWM's legal rights to conduct appeals. This may have been because of fear of the opposition which such a move might have stirred up within the trade union movement.

The NUWM leadership's expertise was certainly acknowledged in some official and academic circles at national level, and this brought pride and pleasure to the movement's leaders. William Beveridge, the 'architect' of the welfare state, asked Hannington and Elias to advise official committees on more than one occasion, and their stay was on at least one occasion much longer than initially envisaged. Although the unemployed movement might be troublesome, it was difficult for serious students to ignore its immense experience and expertise in national insurance questions.

The Communist Party leadership, particularly during the early 1930s, was not impressed by this type of activity, which was severely criticised on the grounds that it was 'legalism' which encouraged 'passivity' and diverted the movement from developing mass agitations. Although it was not generally argued that it should be completely dropped, the view (pushed consistently in the early editions of the *Daily Worker*) was that it should become secondary. The problem with the argument would seem to be that once the procedure was set up, the NUWM had something of an all-or-nothing choice to make: whether to represent people or not. It is difficult to see how it could have become 'secondary'. Hannington's reply to the argument was that whilst there was a danger of the representational work becoming predominant, this was reduced by the branches having specialist committees so that not all of the activists were swamped with this kind of work. But he insisted that the work should be maintained, despite the criticisms of Lewis Jones and Harry Pollitt. It provided the basis for agitation both in terms of building relationships with those represented, and in terms of providing cases for propaganda purposes.[22]

This debate was initiated by the Communist Party, and does not appear to have been reflected at local level. The experience of the movement's members was one of having to battle vigorously to establish the right to representation. They refused to see themselves as 'legalists'. An example should serve to illustrate the point. Those who chaired local insurance appeals tribunals sometimes told claimants that they could only be represented by a 'friend' and not by an NUWM representative. The existence of the NUWM was denied, but, more importantly, the right to appeal was removed. One local claims secretary, Hughes of Kidgrove, was asked whether he appeared as a 'friend'. He replied:

All the workers are my friends and Mr W.Latham was a member of our Organisation. Mr Latham agreed with same but the chairman took exception of myself mentioning Organisation. The chairman asked me to retire from the room. I stated if I went, Comrade Latham would go. Comrade Latham then stated if I went he would go. The proceedings of

the Appeal Tribunal was held up forty-five minutes when the
Police came and the Constable asked me to retire from the
Room.[23]

From this time onwards, Hughes was refused admittance to
represent people, even as a friend. It would probably have
been difficult to persuade him that he was guilty of 'legalism'
or that he was fighting in the wrong arena. His experience
would certainly have made it difficult to make out such an
argument to him.[24]

The way that the system of representation developed
contained important disadvantages for the unemployed
movement which the 'legalism' criticism only partly covered.
The criticism was in one sense difficult to reject, in that it
could hardly be argued that mass agitational work was really
helped by individual representation. Local activists often
complained, like Sid Elias, that they were 'completely
overwhelmed' by paperwork.[25] Clearly, whilst they were doing
paperwork and attending tribunals, they could not be
agitating. Although it was true that tremendous mass
movements were developing whilst representational work
grew, the latter could not be anything but a distraction.
Perhaps, then, there was some justice in the CPGB
leadership's accusation: perhaps the mass movements could
have been even wider. There was another, and in some ways
more important drawback with the legal activity which was
not to do with 'legalism', and this concerned the whole nature
of the NUWM. The fact that a considerable part of the
movement's work involved local branches looking upwards to
the national office for help, advice and direction assisted the
process of centralisation already in train in the NUWM. The
habit of looking towards the national leadership for direction
could not be limited to one area of activity, and power became
increasingly centralised within the organisation. This made it
gradually become more centrally directed and less of a
federation of committees. The leadership often indicated that
it thought this a healthy development, but it had insidious
effects on local militants who were constantly trying to
interpret and implement decisions made at headquarters, or
ignoring them. Either way, their own self-activity was hardly
encouraged. Police spies were also given an easier job.

On the other hand, the representational work had an enormous positive effect on the NUWM, in that it was provided with a major reason for existence by the state itself, since membership either of a trade union or of the NUWM was required if a national insurance appeal was to be entertained. During the 1930s, Labour Exchange officials were known to scrutinise NUWM cards closely to see when the person had joined, and whether he or she was up to date with contributions. Here was an ironic situation! Local government officials were indirectly enforcing NUWM membership. This presented the unemployed movement with an unexpected ally. More importantly, it provided it with a major recruiting argument. Moreover, the representational work provided it with a continuous basis for its activity which its previous agitational work had denied it. In this sense, the movement became more like a trade union, and achieved greater stability. In periods without any mass agitation, there was still an important reason for joining the NUWM.

The Labour Government and the Crisis of 1931

Debates within the NUWM, or between the NUWM and the CPGB, were overshadowed in 1931 by broader upheavals within the whole labour movement, brought on by the economic crisis. During 1930, there had been no great public awareness of the extent and depth of the world economic catastrophe. In April 1930, the government took several steps aimed at ameliorating the position of the workless. But, during 1931, many European banks collapsed completely and the Bank of England had repeatedly to draw on reserves to keep the pound on the gold standard. Unemployment rose rapidly as financial interests launched a campaign to cut public spending and to remove the Labour government. The government was faced with a major dilemma: whether to continue its defence of the interests of the unemployed, or to make cuts at their expense in the hope of remaining in office. The right wing of the Parliamentary Labour Party began to win the upper hand in this discussion. In the summer of 1931, the Anomalies Act took away many people's right to claim. At the end of July, the May Committee reported that the financial position demanded reductions in benefit. The Cabinet split on the issue of the cuts, and the dilemma was brought to a head. Ramsay MacDonald, Snowden and Jimmy Thomas abandoned the Labour Party in favour of a 'National' alliance of all parties in favour of the cuts. In the following General Election, the Labour MPs who remained loyal to the party were in an impossible situation, as they tried to campaign against cuts in benefit whilst their erstwhile leaders opposed them in alliance with the other parties. They were not even generally supported by the NUWM at local level, as NUWM branches were now deeply influenced by the Communist Party's sectarian policy towards the Labour Party. The result was a crushing defeat for Labour. The Labour Party won just 49 seats in the House of Commons, with the rest going to the 'Nationals' in some guise or another. The political wing of the labour movement had suffered a crushing defeat.

The leadership of the unemployed movement regarded these events as proof positive of their analysis of the Labour Party, and of their characterisation of its leaders as 'social fascist'. Here they were betraying the interests of workers in favour of those of the City and international capital. But they could take little comfort in such reflections. The 'National' government now had a clear mandate to proceed to cuts in benefit; there was no longer any question of a serious parliamentary debate on this. There was no possibility of lobbying or embarrassing the government. In this context, the NUWM was now the only recourse for those workless who believed that the cuts could be fought, since the alternatives were so obviously no longer available. But, by the same token, everyone realised that the fight would be especially hard. Whilst the lines of battle were clearly drawn, the unemployed movement was very much at a strategic disadvantage. The development of a mass movement in these circumstances was an achievement which should not be underestimated.

The presence within the NUWM of a strong and cohesive political leadership provided by the Communist Party did at least mean that the movement was alert to the threat posed by the 'National' government. The small band of British Communists was now concentrating its efforts on the NUWM. Victimised out of employment, it was hardly possible for them to be active in their trade unions, and the Minority Movement effectively collapsed during 1931 for this reason. The Communists brought intense activity and a very clear political 'line' with them. There were problems which flowed from this, as Pat Devine pointed out when he said that there was an attitude which was 'rampant' within the Communist Party of seeing political weaknesses in the NUWM which it was the duty of party members to 'smash'. Highly politicised Communists coming into contact with 'green' recruits to the NUWM could demolish the confidence of the unemployed and drive them away.[25] Despite the problems, Communists were very much to the fore at a local level in the early 1930s. At a national level, the Communist leaders were very much in control. The Seventh National Conference, held in February 1931, had elected a triumvirate of Hannington, Elias and the studious South Wales Communist[26] Llewellyn to be a 'National Secretariat' to run the movement between NACs.[27] These three, supported by Tom Mann as Treasurer and Maud Brown as Women's Organiser, formed the group which Hannington thought the most formidable headquarters team ever assembled by the NUWM.

The Cuts Arrive

In August 1931, Hannington consistently warned in the columns of the *Worker* that the new government was about to attack the workless. This was, he argued, by far the most serious situation that had ever confronted the unemployed. The next month his warnings were shown to have been appropriate. Government employees and servicemen suffered pay cuts, sparking off the 'mutiny' in the Home Fleet at Invergordon. But the most vicious attacks were on the unemployed. The government issued two Orders in Council, the first to take effect on 5 October and the second from 12 November. The first order increased contributions to the Unemployment Insurance Scheme, and reduced benefits by 10 per cent. The second order, although apparently more technical, was in many respects more damaging. It limited the period for receipt of statutory unemployment benefit to 26 weeks in a benefit year, and imposed a Family Means Test on all who continued to be out of work. By these two measures, nearly 400,000 claimants were immediately removed from statutory benefit, which was theirs by right, and became instead 'transitional' claimants under the jurisdiction of the new Public Assistance Committees.

These claimants joined the large number of people already in the same situation, who were now threatened with the Family Means Test. Whilst non-insurance benefits had always been means-tested, the new measure was a devastating one. The Family Means Test was at the centre of the unemployed movement's agitations during the 1930s, just as the Not Genuinely Seeking Work clause had been in the 1920s. It meant that it was the responsibility of every claimant to give full details of the income of every member of his or her family, under threat of prosecution. The total weekly income of the family was then worked out, and the amount by which it was greater than Poor Law Relief was then deducted from the claimant's benefit. In many cases, this meant that the claimant was entitled to nothing. Hannington gave the example of a young man living with his parents. The man had been unemployed for over 26 weeks, and the family was therefore means-tested. The assessment of the family's relief entitlement was 30s. per week. Since the father earned 31s. per week, the son was entitled to nothing, and had to be kept by his father.[28]

The Means Test applied to 852,000 claimants when it was introduced, and Hannington argued that its impact was more serious than the 10 per cent cuts. As ever, he showed by this assessment how close he was to the feelings of the unemployed. People felt that financial hardship was being accompanied by the degrading and humiliating process of a state inquiry into the financial means of the whole family. Many deeply resented being forced into total dependency on their relatives, not necessarily related by blood. In many cases, young men felt that they had little alternative but to leave home so that they would not be considered 'dependent'. Many therefore became homeless. As desperate people, the family had often been their only source of comfort and affection. Not a few people felt driven to the point at which they took their own lives as the only way out.

The NUWM publicised such cases as part of their campaign against the new measures, but they emphasised to the workless that suicide was not the direction to take.

Unemployed demonstrators jumping out of commandeered lorries during a police charge on the 1932 Hunger March

Women marchers leaving London for the Brighton TUC, 1 September 1933

NUWM demonstration in Birkenhead, 1936

Demonstrators chained to railings at Stepney Labour Exchange, 1938

NUWM demonstrators outside Victoria Station as Chamberlain left for Rome, 10 January 1939

Wal Hannington addressing inmates outside Kielder Camp, 1939

NUWM meeting in Trafalgar Square, 5 February 1939

NUWM members conducting a mock fishing tournament in waterlogged trenches on Primrose Hill, London, February 1939

Personal 'solutions' of any sort were not the way forward. The unemployed should not turn in on themselves, but ought to understand that the capitalist system was to blame. As Eddie Jones, a NUWM activist from South Wales, argued in a speech for which his notes survive, it was not simply a question of capitalism choking on its own wasteful over-production. The British government had sufficient money; it was paying out £200 million to bondholders on the National Debt every year, to 'fill the pockets of people who were the real gainers from the last war'.[29] The new measures brought increasing numbers of people to think that there was something in what the NUWM said; whilst not necessarily accepting the movement's arguments in their entirety, many people felt inclined to follow its lead. With alternative opportunities such as casual and 'black economy' work at an all-time low, many of the young men decided to throw in their lot with the NUWM. Mass upheavals were the result. By the beginning of October 1931, the *Worker* went so far as to say that the unemployed were recreating their rebellion of the early 1920s. This upsurge was of large proportions, and lasted through most of the winter, to fall away again in the early summer of 1932.[30]

New Recruits, New Battles

Large demonstrations were held in all major towns even before the week ending 9 October, when the cuts took place. In November, Means Test forms were issued to claimants, and the NUWM responded by organising marches to return the forms. Marches to the PACs, to factories to hold factory-gate meetings and to the workhouses were being organised all over the country. Throughout the autumn, reports flooded in of action being taken by practically every NUWM branch. There were sizeable demonstrations even in small towns: in Accrington, for example, there was a demonstration of about 2,500 against the cuts and the Means Test.

The NUWM was at the head of a continuous ferment of unrest, which involved large numbers of people during any given week of that winter. The General Election saw leading members of the movement standing for the Communist Party, with Hannington contesting West Bermondsey and McShane the Gorbals, but their campaigns were simply a tiny part of a much more extensive and turbulent battle. By the time the election took place in October, mass involvement was developing. The nature of the demonstrations of this time is perhaps best described by an excellent working-class writer who participated in one. In *I Was One Of The Unemployed,* Max Cohen tells of how, on his way to the Labour Exchange in a town he called 'Forgeton', he saw large crowds of men gathered in one street. Asking a man what the crowd was there for, and learning that they were getting ready for a demonstration, he decided to join them. Leaving the Labour Exchange after the march had started, he caught it up by taking a tram:

> The tram reached the centre of the town. There had been no sign of the marchers. The tram proceeded down the main street, and suddenly I beheld a spectacle which electrified me. It seemed as though a mighty flood of people stretched down the street, into the distance, as far as the eye could see. I had never seen such a large crowd. The black flood surged impetuously towards the direction from which the tram was coming. It was a black flood flecked with red – red banners on which were slogans with white letters. Everybody on top of the tram car was standing up, craning eagerly in the direction of the demonstrators, gazing with wonderment and incredulity.
>
> Suddenly, more astonishing than the pouring stream of people, a vast elemental roar smote the sky, re-echoed and vibrated from the tall buildings.
> 'Not-a-penny-off-the-dole!'
> 'Not-a-man-off-benefit!'
> 'Down-with-the-Means-Test!'
> I got off the tram-car just before the demonstration reached it. For a moment I hesitated on the pavement as the river of people swept past me, and then I plunged into it.
> It was not without a certain feeling of strangeness that I slipped into the ranks of the demonstrators and found myself marching with people I had never seen before.
> The demonstration surged irresistibly through the heart of the city. Crowds of well-dressed people, of the type who spend their afternoons shopping or visiting places of amusement, stood on the pavement and gaped at this unprecedented spectacle.

We turned to march through the commercial and business section of the town. There were large, high blocks of offices in these streets, and as we marched along, every window up to the highest storey was crowded with office-workers gazing down in astonishment. Accompanying the marchers were a number of collectors of funds from the National Unemployed Workers' Movement, which had arranged the march. As the collectors rattled their boxes, showers of coins descended from even the highest windows, and the collectors were kept busy hunting for them.

By now I had recovered from my first strangeness in taking part in the demonstration and began to look about me. I saw many of the marchers carrying posters nailed to short sticks. On the posters were various slogans:

Work or full maintenance!
Not a penny off the dole!
Not a man off benefit!
Down with the Means Test!

The tramp of thousands of feet seemed to make the very roadway tremble and vibrate. The roar of shouted slogans crashed against the walls of the office buildings and thundered against the sky. The police and inspectors who accompanied us were politeness and courtesy personified. They held up the traffic to allow us to proceed without difficulty and without pausing. Press photographers, perched high on the tops of buildings, photographed the march as it passed by. Wherever the march passed, there the life of the town seemed to be held up whilst thousands thronged the pavements and crowded to windows to see the demonstration.

Finally we reached the conclusion of the march, and the demonstration wound up as a protest meeting against the new Unemployment Act and the Means Test. A vast sea of people listened to the speakers, who appeared tiny, puppet-like by comparison with their enormous audience. We dispersed from the meeting with the confident feeling that such an enormous demonstration could not but have the effect of bringing our case before the public and the government in no uncertain manner. We dispersed with optimism, sure of victory.[31]

Cohen's descriptive powers evoke with startling immediacy the feeling of being caught up in a movement much bigger than himself. The strength of popular support for the demonstrators helped to ensure that the police were on this occasion friendly, but in the next demonstration he describes, they were much more hostile and attacked the marchers with batons.

Police attacks were a common feature of the demonstrations of late 1931. The demonstrations held in Salford and Manchester were in fact the most violent and bloody unemployed conflicts of the inter-war period, certainly in the greater Manchester area. In Salford, on 1 October several thousand people, including many women, demonstrated outside the Town Hall, with the aim of persuading the Town Council to oppose the cuts and the Means Test. Marching in columns of four, the marchers broke through a police cordon intended to divert them from taking their planned route. There appears to have been, as so often during this wave of action, a good deal of support for the unemployed amongst the onlookers, but this did not prevent the police from attacking them in Bexley Square. Many were arrested and others, like Communist NUWM member Eddie Frow were badly beaten in police custody. George Watson, secretary of the Salford NUWM, was arrested with several close comrades.[32] Six days later, a crowd of more than 20,000 including many who had joined the demonstrators as they proceeded, fought bitterly with the police in Central Manchester. Banned from holding their meeting in Albert Square, one of the leaders was starting to address the crowd when the police charged. The *Manchester Guardian* reported the following day:

> In a second the cross-roads were a welter of fighting men, of horses pushing through the struggling confusion, of policemen hitting right and left with batons, of marchers retaliating with stout sticks to which their placards had been nailed, with stones, bricks, lumps of coke. Firemen appeared and a couple of horses quartered the crowd like machine guns spraying water. In an incredibly short space of time after the sudden breakdown of endurance, it was possible to see the cross-roads. Broken banners, broken stocks, a wash of water, a litter of hats, caps and helmets met the eye, with here and there a man lying.[33]

On 8 October, 38 people were tried on various charges arising out of the Salford disturbances, and a large number of police saturated the area around the two courts. The sentences ranged from five months to being bound over, but they were not announced until the day after all the defendants had been tried, apparently for fear of the reaction which they might provoke.[34] The sentences had a serious effect on the NUWM, as virtually the entire local leadership had been taken out of circulation at a stroke. It was left to Larry Finlay, an unemployed Communist engineer, to carry on the agitation. As a good Communist, he took up the challenge, but such thorough repression inevitably had a dampening effect on the movement locally.[35]

The situation was similar throughout urban Britain in early October. Disturbances in Glasgow led to the arrest and imprisonment of a number of activists, although Harry McShane kept out of prison by defending himself ably in court. In London, Hannington had already been arrested for disturbing the peace and incitement when he called on the unemployed to demonstrate in support of others already arrested for their part in an earlier demonstration to the House of Commons. Four days after Hannington's arrest, Elias was imprisoned for one month. Nor were all of these arrests the result of mass demonstrations; many came from quite normal NUWM activity. In London, many arrests followed on the decision of Lord Trenchard (the Metropolitan Police Commissioner) that no meetings were to be held outside Labour Exchanges. In Plumstead, William Masheder, an ex-miner, was imprisoned for refusing to be bound over after refusing to lead an NUWM group out of a PAC meeting.[36]

With large numbers of people being drawn into the protests, rocketing unemployment and the growth of the NUWM, the National government was having recourse to naked repression. The government, having been formed to cut, was proceeding with its policy, and simply suppressed the opposition without making any concessions. Despite some local victories of a minor type, there were few gains from this wave of agitation. One or two PACs, like St Pancras, pledged themselves to pay full benefit to all those coming under the Means Test, but the national situation remained the same.[37] In a sense, the official policy was working. It has been suggested that the violence surrounding the 1931 demonstrations alienated many people from the politics of protest. Many were horrified at the level of violence, and although some realised that it had not all been the fault of the NUWM, had no wish to become involved in anything which might lead to violent confrontation, this was one of the factors in causing the agitation to fall away.[38] The most widespread and intense actions had ended by mid-November, and were followed by a few months of less dramatic protest until the spring.

The wave of protest swelled the ranks of the unemployed movement. By December 1931, there were about 35,000 members organised in over 300 branches.[39] Perhaps more importantly, the movement had succeeded in gaining some wider sympathy for its campaign against the Means Test. This in turn encouraged the Communist Party to begin to move away from the more destructive aspects of its 'Third Period' political line. The process was a gradual one, and would not be complete for several years, but it was set in train in January 1932. Harry Pollitt presented a statement entitled 'The Turn to Mass Work' to the party's Political Bureau at the end of 1931, which then submitted it to the Central Committee. This paper stressed, amongst other things, the importance of working in the trade unions.[40] There is no doubt that Pollitt's argument strengthened those Communists who wished to work in the existing unions. In May 1932 the NUWM organised a Conference Against the Means Test, which attracted 679 delegates from NUWM and trade union bodies, and decided on another Hunger March.[41]

Unemployed Councils: A Blind Alley

One aspect of the 'turn to mass work' within the Communist Party had quite negative effects within the NUWM. This was the idea of Unemployed Councils, which although initially not coming from the Communist Party, was nevertheless pushed by it as a form of mass work.

The idea originated with the international communist trade union body, the Red International of Labour Unions (RILU), in 1931. Broad committees of the unemployed were to be set up based not on membership of any unemployed organisation, but simply on the willingness to fight of those involved. First publicised in Britain through the *Worker* in the summer of 1931, the idea was to pull in all the unemployed by breaking down the 'barrier' represented by the NUWM, through elections to the Council held at mass meetings outside Labour Exchanges. Financial contributions would only be expected on a voluntary basis, and not in the form of a regular subscription as in the NUWM.[42] The Unemployed Councils were far from successful in Britain; despite strong and sometimes recriminatory appeals from the leadership, the rank and file saw no particular reason for these bodies and so only implemented the tactic in a desultory fashion. The episode has been presented by one historian as a 'failure' which showed the problems the NAC faced in getting the membership to put policies into practice. From the perspective of the NAC, this is quite accurate; from another perspective, that of the best interests of the NUWM as an organisation, it could be seen quite differently: as the membership saving the NUWM from its Communist-dominated leadership by passive resistance.[43]

After an initial series of articles in the *Worker* explaining RILU's idea, items by Hannington, Elias and McShane were published in an attempt to cajole, persuade and inspire the activists to action.[44] The leaders of the unemployed movement by and large simply reproduced the arguments of the RILU, that institutional conservatism should be cast aside, that new recruits would bring new strength, and so on. But perhaps the most significant aspect of these articles was the way that they revealed the arguments of their opponents, who had no public voice in these discussions. Sid Elias, for example, reported on discussions that he had with the Nottinghamshire and Derby District Council of the NUWM in December 1931. The principal problem, as seen by 'many comrades' was that 'the establishment of broad committees would lead to the present members of the NUWM throwing up membership and simply becoming a part of the broad committee without membership conditions'.[45] Similar objections were reported by Hannington and McShane. None of their answers were very convincing: Elias argued that the building of the new committees 'should not be interpreted in any mechanical way', whilst Hannington and McShane claimed that the new bodies would not be rivals at all, but, as Hannington said, 'an adjunct which would enable us to develop the struggle'.[46]

Experience proved the local activists right. In two cases, in Springburn in Scotland and Great Harwood in Lancashire, confusion between the new Unemployed Council and the NUWM branch led to the complete collapse of both.[47] Yet this did not prevent the NAC from castigating the branches as a whole for not taking the idea up. There was, they said in May 1932, 'a very serious lack of responsiveness to these headquarters' decisions and directives which result often in no attempt whatever to operate the leads and in others a very half-hearted and slow application of the lines of work'. [48] If there had been problems in practice, it was because the line was not being applied correctly.

These 'failures' were regarded with displeasure by Moscow. But an opportunity to 'improve' the situation was offered in 1932. Sid Elias had been elected top of the poll at the 1931 NUWM Conference to travel to RILU, where he was to work in the English-speaking section of the organisation then headed by Lozovsky. Trips to Moscow were then a favourite device on the part of the Comintern and RILU for obtaining reports from non-Soviet Communists, and for reinforcing Moscow lines which were being inadequately applied in practice. In the summer of 1932, substantial articles began to appear in the British Communist press on the subject of unemployed councils. A letter from the European Secretariat of the RILU to the NUWM stressed the need to build Unemployed Councils in July 1932.[49] A fortnight later, F.Emmerich carried on the drive by analysing European unemployed movements in a way that hardly flattered the NUWM. In Germany, Emmerich noted, there were 2,600 unemployed councils; in Czechoslovakia 1,600, and in Britain only five or six. This was ascribed to 'sectarian resistance' to the idea in Britain and the USA.[50] Only a few months later, the NAC pointed out that Emmerich had in fact been wrong: there were no unemployed councils in existence in Britain.[51]

The whole episode had been quite damaging to the unemployed movement. At a time when the unemployed faced very serious attacks, there was no spare time or energy to be dissipated in activities which simply resulted in frustrating and demoralising experiences for which activists were then blamed. Locally, it was appreciated that there were at least two key problems with the council strategy: subscriptions, and establishing a clear role for the councils. As far as subscriptions were concerned, there was certainly some force

in the argument that unemployed people might prefer to join
an unemployed council and pay when they liked, than join the
NUWM which attempted to enforce regular subscriptions.
But the most telling point was that relating to the role of the
unemployed councils. The NUWM was not some sort of
forbiddingly bureaucratic organisation which repelled those
wishing to join it by means of artificial barriers to
membership. If many of the workless did not join it, it was not
because there was obstruction by 'officials'. There was
therefore no real role for a wider, less formalised body. The
NUWM was precisely such a body itself. It was hardly
surprising if those who had devoted their energy to building
the NUWM showed little enthusiasm for the new councils.

A revealing aspect of the experiment was the way in which
the rank and file of the NUWM made these points to the
leadership, but were effectively ignored. The policy had come
from the RILU, was pushed by the leadership and resisted by
the membership. The leaders, disappointed by the results,
then berated the activists and identified the latter's arguments
as reasons for the policy's failure. It was a classic case of the
relationship between the international Communist movement
and grass-roots militants of the period. The 'line' eventually
changed not because of pressure from below but because the
Communist International altered its tactics after the Nazis
seized power in Germany.

Whilst the leaders of the NUWM had been urging the
unemployed councils on branches, massive agitations had
been taking place. A National Day of Struggle was held on 23
February 1932, which the NAC praised as having 'reached a
very high stage'. Particularly large demonstrations had been
held in Bristol and Manchester, whilst in a number of places
longstanding police bans on demonstrating had been
successfully defied. A particularly positive feature of the action
was 'the bringing to the forefront of local issues and in this
way getting the unemployed to recognise that the NUWM
was their movement and not a movement imposed upon them
in a purely dictatorial manner from above'.[52] The NAC was
showing that whilst it was not prepared to brook opposition to
its general policies, it was pleased to see the movement giving
national agitations a local dimension.

National and Local Newspapers of the NUWM

The NAC felt that a national newspaper was essential to build awareness of the national unemployed movement. This had always been the case, but by the spring of 1932 it felt that there was sufficient membership and interest to make an attempt at publishing a newspaper. It began cautiously, 'launching a campaign' by collecting material and selecting worker correspondents before it took the plunge. The paper was to begin on a monthly basis, with the aim of converting to a fortnightly after a short time.[53] *Unemployed Special* appeared as planned, on 16 July 1932. It was an eight-page tabloid-size costing one penny and printed by Utopia Press. From the third issue the editor (after his release from prison) was Pat Devine, who asserted the independence of the paper in his first editorial, stressing that 'although the NUWM is responsible for the *Special* we are not a home organ'.[54] The paper was intended, then, to be one with which the unemployed generally could identify. But the problem was to be, as with all unemployed papers, that the circulation remained small and the finances precarious. The first two editions sold only around 15,000. A change of name was attempted after four issues, the new paper being called *Unemployed Leader*. Although there was a brief flurry of fortnightly editions, from January 1933 the paper had to return to being a monthly. At its meeting held in February 1933, the NAC heard of sales of 19,000 and a debt of £174.[55] In May, the paper was reduced to a small duplicated bulletin containing mainly legal information on benefit questions. In November 1933, it was restored to a printed format, and printed editions appeared most months until November 1935.

The revival of a national newspaper, in however sporadic a form, was very welcome to the membership, which often voiced its appreciation. The papers of the 1930s performed a very useful function of reporting local activities and (a particular feature of these papers) presenting factual and statistical items on legal and benefit questions. In this sense, the *Unemployed Leader* was an educator in a way that had not been true of earlier, more propagandistic publications. The needs of the movement had changed, and so had the papers. But, all too often, the *Unemployed Leader* addressed the reader in a manner uncomfortably reminiscent of Comintern communications. This could even be true of the way that the editors dealt with letters, which reappeared in the paper in July 1934. The following month a reader from Coatbridge wrote in lambasting his own NUWM branch for not selling sufficient copies of the *Unemployed Leader*. The editor, not content to let the criticism rest there, decided to 'reply' to this criticism by adding one of his own. The German comrades, he pointed out, were risking their lives to distribute the Communist *Die Rote Fahne*; in comparison, 'our task is a small one ...'[56] This sort of dialogue could hardly be expected to interest the average unemployed worker, and helps to explain the relative unpopularity of the 1930s papers when set beside the *Out Of Work* of the early 1920s.

Nevertheless, the emphasis placed on 'direct approaches' to the unemployed during the early 1930s bore considerable fruit in a crop of good local newspapers. These were generally lively and down-to-earth in their approach, if understandably poorly produced and short lived. In August 1933, for example, the West Fife District Council of the NUWM published the first issue of its duplicated paper, the *Unemployed Demonstrator*. The paper seems to have had a number of functions for its area: it drummed up support for a forthcoming regional march, publicised a meeting to be held with Harry McShane and John McGovern, and printed the demands of the NUWM. It also whipped up feeling against domestic service, saying

> We have recently had cases in which girls were expected to sleep in old garages which 'the mistress' referred to as a 'bungalow'. Every girl should be on her guard as it is clear that rotten employers are using the Exchange to force girls to accept rotten conditions. Report at once to the NUWM.[57]

In the second edition, Communist Party politics came through clearly with an attack on the TUC for co-operating with the 'Boss Class', behaviour which was contrasted with the fighting stance adopted by the NUWM, which was referred to as 'the Union'. In all the surviving copies, one can trace development of the theme of capitalism giving rise to a ridiculous and contradictory state of affairs: whilst millions were starving, essential foods were being destroyed to keep prices high. But the paper was not simply a propaganda organ. It also fulfilled a vital function for the unemployed. Each edition contained an item of very carefully and clearly explained information, helping people through the complexities of the benefits system. Typical cases were used to show the key principles, precisely how to claim was explained, and scales of relief were reproduced. The importance of this kind of information can hardly be overstated. Then, as now, many people simply did not understand their rights under the system, and how benefit was calculated. They therefore had little choice but to accept the rulings handed down to them. The paper, one of a number of local papers published during the 1930s, most of which seem to have sold for one penny, was, therefore, of immediate use to its readers.

Arthur Speight is Killed

The summer of 1932 saw a high level of activity. There was no 'summer slump', or period of slackness which usually occurred during the better weather. This was a sign that the depth of feeling against the Means Test was sufficient to ensure a continuous wave of protest for some time to come. In a number of areas, large scale demonstrations occurred for the first time. These left hundreds injured and imprisoned, and at least one man dead.

In Castleford in Yorkshire, a series of demonstrations in a previously quiet area culminated in a serious outbreak of police violence. During a demonstration to the PAC, the Labour representatives on the PAC voted against receiving a delegation from the unemployed and that evening the unemployed demonstrated to the Trades and Labour Council in protest at the attitude of the Labour representatives. When the Council broke up, shouting at the Labour men became hostile, and police (mainly from outlying districts) made a fierce baton charge which left women, men and children badly hurt and an NUWM member, Arthur Speight, dead. Several local leaders of the movement were arrested, and the following day the Labour magistrate refused to grant any adjournment to the severely injured defendants, and proceeded to sentence them immediately. The NUWM was understandably outraged. Speight's death was taken up as a national issue, many of the members of the movement recognising the intensity of police violence from their own experience. Here, however, was a case of an altogether different sort which greatly increased the feeling in the NUWM against the police, the Labour Party and the National government. Others had died before as a more indirect result of the struggle: Speight, an ordinary member of the NUWM, had died from an 'egg-shaped' head wound. In the demonstrations which followed during the autumn, NUWM banners were often draped with black in memory of Arthur Speight. The NAC stressed that the appropriate response was to intensify the agitation.[58]

Climax of Struggle: Birkenhead

In late May 1932, the National Conference Against the Means Test had resolved to launch another Hunger March. As final preparations for the march were under way in September, a tremendous wave of unemployed revolt swept through numerous British towns. On 6 September, a big demonstration to the Council took place in Bristol; that same day, thousands marched in Motherwell, Port Glasgow and Birkenhead. On 10 September, there was a large 'united front' conference to begin a new campaign, further demonstrations in Bristol and large demonstrations organised by the NUWM with the left-wing United Mineworkers of Scotland. But the most serious battles were yet to come. As in Castleford, the police reaction was extreme.

On 13 September, about 10,000 unemployed marched to the Birkenhead PAC to present a set of demands, the main element in which was a three shilling per week increase in the scales of relief. The PAC promised to consider these demands. As the deputation returned to the demonstration, and the crowd began to disperse, the police attacked the march and several people were arrested. Another demonstration was held two days later to demand the release of those arrested. On this occasion, police drafted in from other areas attacked the march, and pitched battles ensued, resulting in many injuries to the unemployed. The following day, there was another demonstration and further fighting; during that night, the police came round working-class areas smashing windows and assaulting those who they thought had been involved in the demonstrations. The whole NUWM branch committee was arrested. Similar scenes were enacted the following night. By the fourth day of the fighting, the Birkenhead PAC made some concessions: the weekly relief scales were raised by 3s 3d for men and 3s 6d for women. The Town Council established public works schemes at trade union rates of pay to the value of £180,000. These were considerable advances, but the price was high. 45 unemployed people were tried after these 'riots'; two local NUWM leaders received sentences of two years.[59]

Such is the outline history of the Birkenhead disturbances. But the account of a participant can be set beside it. This is the story as told by the late John Jackson, at that time a young Catholic member of the NUWM's Birkenhead branch. Jackson had been a member of the Wallasey Unemployed Association, which affiliated to the NUWM. As a Catholic, he had been brought up to think of Communists as the 'Anti-Christ', but he had also acquired a sense of social morality which allowed him to see the force of their arguments when he was unemployed. He found the facts and figures produced by the NUWM in support of their case irrefutable, and became an enthusiastic member. As a young man with no family responsibilities, he, along with many others involved, was philosophical about being arrested; and about imprisonment: 'If you got put away, you got put away.' Half a century later, he recalled some of his experiences in the Birkenhead events. He insisted on beginning by describing how those in authority saw the workless:

> The *Daily Worker* brought out a list of the requirements of the unemployed, and the working classes, and to test your MP with these doings, and Moore-Brabazon was the MP for Wallasey and we tackled him on this and his wife speaking in support of him said that any woman worth her salt could keep a man for 15s 3d a week. And so about 500 of us in the town, we went to her for adoption, we asked her to adopt us. When I say 500 I may be exaggerating, there was quite a crowd of the unemployed ... and chaps saying, 'You can have me family as well, if you like ...' *But this was attitude, that 15s 3d was a lot of money!* The man who was in charge of the National Assistance Board, he was on ninety pounds a week, that was his wages, his salary, we were on 15s 3d and he was telling us how to live.

This was the sort of thing you were getting from them, people telling you how you'd got to be contented, and how they were reducing the unemployed. Of course they were reducing the unemployed, when you got thrown off the Means Test you never bothered going along any more, so you were just wiped out, and this went on for so long, to me now it's funny. But in those days when I was young and idealistic, to see kids going to school in their bare feet, was heart-breaking, and I saw it, so much of it ...

[The police] had no sympathy for you in Liverpool, the police, well, I sometimes think that they glorified in the fact that they could draw their sticks on the unemployed. In Birkenhead, they read the Riot Act on the Town Hall steps one night, and Joe Rawlings, Eugene Coffee, and a woman, what was her name, Mrs ... they had a march down to the Town Hall. A person named Mrs Gossage was the chairman of the parish relief. First of all they had a meeting at the park entrance in Birkenhead, that's the Hyde Park Corner of Birkenhead, and the meeting passed a resolution, like they do, that the meeting would march on the home of this Mrs Gossage. As they tried to form up, so the coppers moved in and they started. There was no argument about it, it was the Birmingham 'A' Division, they were the SAS, the riot breakers of the police force ... then about two or three nights there was rioting going on throughout the town. People would say, 'What have I done, you're not smashing my window' because they wanted the insurance money ... and the police were so much about it that at night time around the park entrance at Birkenhead was what in those days was one of the real slum areas of Birkenhead, not only was it a slum area, it was an Irish Catholic area, and on the night time the police came up there with their sticks drawn shouting, 'Come out, you Irish bastards, come out, come out, face us.' Anything to egg the people to come out and have a go, so that they could do something. I've got a scar here [pointing to his head, R.C.]. Between Birkenhead and where I lived, I had to go over the docks, the Birkenhead docks, what we called the four bridges, and every one of them bridges was manned, and I tried to go home the next day, and they was still searching. Again, you see, the thing got out of hand because the chaps weren't sort of fighting the police, they were knocking the shops. It's understandable, but the Co-op shop got done, the grocer's shop, but they didn't do it for the food in it, they would just throw it about. But the unemployed themselves, the genuine unemployed, the genuine protesters, this wasn't their action, this was the action of the skinheads of the day, who'd seen an opportunity to go in and get something, you know, jewellers' shops and such like. I remember, it'd be about three o'clock in the morning, outside the Co-op shop in Livingstone Street, I'd seen chaps playing bowls with tins of salmon ... nobody seemed to have enough sympathy for the unemployed, to come to the unemployed and say, 'Look, we can understand your plight and we can understand your feeling,' but with the coppers it was stick, stick, stick, you know there was no arguing, there was no arguing about it, it was just stick, and you know I could never understand it because they were just working-class people. The coppers on the horses with their three foot sticks, they were really tremendous. They were swinging them as they went by you, through you. They weren't asking you to clear the pathway, they cleared it ... I was speaking at a place we called the 'Guinea Gap' and they was holding a meeting, you know, an unemployed meeting, and in the local newspaper they mentioned the fact that the Duke of Westminster's yacht was to come through the Mersey, on the way to Eden Hall, his home near Chester, and that he'd bought his wife a necklace, a diamond necklace that had cost £200,000. And I mentioned this fact when I was speaking. I said, 'You know, isn't it marvellous, I can't buy a packet of Woodbines, and yet this guy can have this yacht going through and buy his wife a necklace for £200,000. Wonder what's wrong? And a tap on the shoulder says to me, 'If you don't stop that, you'll find out.' The copper was warning me that I'd got to the point where he was going to do me if I didn't shut up.[60]

John Jackson's account of the Birkenhead 'riots' began and ended with incidents which for him epitomised the inequalities within British society of the time. In this context, he found the looting which went on in these disturbances understandable, though not an act of genuine protest. Looting was a feature of many of the disturbances of the early 1930s, and the NUWM always took this attitude to it. It tended, however, to help those who would like to brand all unemployed protesters as criminals, and to justify the intensity of the police response to such demonstrators.

The Belfast Disturbances

One of the interesting features of Jackson's account of the 'Birkenhead riots' was the emphasis he put on police violence against the Irish Catholics in the area. The heavy involvement of the Birkenhead Catholics, and the violent police reaction to it, did not escape the attention of their counterparts in Northern Ireland, where dramatic struggles began just a few days later.

The position with relief in Northern Ireland was different to that in the rest of Britain. In Northern Ireland, the Guardians had not been abolished, because the 1929 legislation did not apply. A Public Assistance Committee was established in Belfast, but as a sub-committee of the Poor Law Guardians. The Guardians, always mindful of the effect of higher relief on their rates, followed a particularly parsimonious policy, and allowed relief only to those who qualified under the 1929 Act. Relief was fixed at the very low level of 24s. maximum, irrespective of the number of dependents of the claimant. Also, the administration of relief occurred in the context of the Northern Irish sectarian state. Protestant supremacy meant that Catholics were hit harder by unemployment, and treated worse when they were out of work, than Protestants; such differential treatment was structured in to the very existence and fabric of Northern Ireland. Here, then, was a quite different context to that of the mainland: one of extreme poverty and religious discrimination.[61] The Belfast PAC contributed a third factor to the situation which, whilst not unique, ensured an explosive response which crossed the religious divide. The PAC insisted in all cases on task work if the unemployed were to receive outdoor relief. They thereby grouped together large numbers of unskilled workers, predominantly but not exclusively Catholic. The relief workers were a fertile field for agitation by the small local Unemployed Workers' Movement, which was able to organise a strike of 2,000 relief workers. Moreover, the concern of the trade unions at the large scale of relief work ensured that, in contrast to the situation on the mainland, the unions were prepared to offer support in terms of industrial action.

Soon after the strike began, minor concessions were offered by the Mayor of Belfast, and were rejected. Led by the local Communists, including the young, able and passionate Betty Sinclair, the unemployed knew they could do better, and a series of demonstrations followed. Jack McGougan, recalling these demonstrations, regarded them from his viewpoint as a non-Communist socialist and white-collar employee, as 'very disorganised, they didn't walk in military ranks or anything, they went in surges ...'[62] However disorganised the demonstrations may have been from McGougan's point of view, the unemployed were far from disorganised in a political sense. On 10 October, the Relief Workers' Strike Committee called for a rent and school strike. The next day, fierce fighting broke out between the police and the unemployed. Two people were shot dead and fifteen received gunshot wounds from the police; a curfew was imposed and British troops were brought into the fray. Large numbers were injured in the ensuing violence. Support then came from the trade unions, and a mass meeting in the linen mills voted for strike action, other unions pledged similar action and the Belfast Trades Council called for a General Strike. On 14 October, the funeral of one of those killed in the fighting took place, attended by Tom Mann, the veteran socialist and NUWM Treasurer, who was arrested and deported. On that day, large increases in the rates of relief were conceded: the rate for a man and wife, for example, was raised from 8s to 20s per week.[63]

The Belfast victory represented a large step forward for the unemployed movement as a whole. Although at the beginning of the dispute, the local unemployed organisation had no real links with the NUWM, this had changed only a few weeks later. More importantly, the system of relief in Northern Ireland had been restructured to the great benefit of the workless, thereby showing what could be achieved elsewhere. The NAC of the NUWM was in no doubt on this count:

> These events in Belfast, coming after Birkenhead and the big fights in the other centres, had a magnificent rallying effect throughout the whole of Britain and unquestionably helped forward the agitation in all parts, particularly in connection with the campaign for extra winter relief.[64]

It is not necessary to accept the argument made out ever since the beginning of the Belfast events that they had opened a 'new era' in Irish history in which class unity would overcome the sectarian divisions between Protestants and Catholics, to see that the limited and temporary unity achieved scared the Northern Irish authorities into making large concessions.[65] The Unionist politicians exerted their influence on the PAC to re-establish the divide by making concessions.[66] The peculiar situation in the province had in this sense helped the workless to move forward, but there was another crucial element in the situation: the strong possibility of support from the employed working class. The threat of action had been on a scale that made it unique in the inter-war period. It is instructive that it brought such dramatic results.

The 1932 Hunger March

The 1932 Hunger March began at the end of September, when the Scottish contingent set off. The total number of unemployed involved was large: about 1,500 were descending on London from various parts of Britain. The marchers took a petition to London which was signed by more than 1,000,000 people. The spirit on the march was excellent. Harry McShane recalled almost fifty years later that: 'You knew you were one of them, and that they were going to go with you through everything.'[67] There was a women's contingent again, as there had been in 1930. The marchers were young, and were soon caught up in the spirit of the march and the movement that had organised it.

The march, in common with other marches, fulfilled a vitally important function for the NUWM, in helping to further the political development of those who went on it. In this way it built up the body of activists, a very important consideration for a movement which needed constant renewal. Dora Cox recalled how effective the march was for women from South Wales. The women developed through their discussions and experiences on the march so that, by its end, several who had never before spoken in public were able to describe what unemployment meant to them and their families. When they arrived in London, the process continued as Frida Laski came to speak to some of the women about visiting a birth control clinic, many of whom went despite reservations.[68]

The young marchers experienced what many others were experiencing in a more limited way in these years when the NUWM was at the centre of a mass movement. They felt that sense of belonging, of exaltation at being part of something much bigger than themselves, which contrasted so dramati-

cally with the isolation and misery of their everyday lives.
Once powerless, they were now part of a disciplined, militant
collective. The marchers were aware of being members of an
elite, chosen for their physical, personal and political qualities
to participate in carrying through the demanding task of
reaching London despite the opposition of those in authority.
They were told of their historic responsibility to the
working-class movement by their leaders. Fortified by the
radical oratory of McShane, Hannington and others, they
faced their responsibilities with determination. Now they were
going to carry the slogans and banners of the NUWM to the
heart of government. The NAC later praised their dedication
in the highest terms: the march had been 'a tremendous
advance on all previous marches organised by the NUWM'.[69]
The marchers could be proud of themselves, especially in view
of the formidable forces ranged against them.

The National government was strongly of the opinion that
the marchers should be harshly treated, and felt that it had a
mandate for the cuts and the Means Test by virtue of its large
parliamentary majority. The march was not sponsored or
supported by any MPs (at the wish of the NUWM), and the
Communist Party was isolated even within the labour
movement. The result was that the 1932 march was the most
brutally treated of all. From the beginning the government was
clearly intent on battering the participants whilst portraying
them as criminals and Communists financed by Moscow.

The Ministry of Health circulated a memorandum to its
General Inspectors which made it quite clear that no effort
was to be spared to prevent anything likely to encourage the
marchers, and it was felt that the structural changes in the
administration of relief would make this easier. The women's
contingent was faced at Burton-on-Trent with the demand
that the marchers should give their names, which they refused
to do. The Lancashire contingent fought a fierce fight with
police in the Stratford-on-Avon Workhouse yard. But the
famous fights of 27 October, in and around Hyde Park, were
the abiding memory of many marchers. Fifteen demonstrators
were injured and fourteen arrested; footage by an amateur
photographer, recently rediscovered, clearly show the police
attacking without provocation.[70] There was further fighting
with the police three days later, and yet more fighting when

the police seized the national petition.

The 1932 march made only minimal gains for the workless, which was hardly surprising given the political context. Whilst some tiny changes were made in the legislation, the main result of the protests was to induce the government to try to promote a quiescent alternative to the NUWM, by funding voluntary organisations to establish unemployed clubs and meeting places. Moreover, the funding idea was presented along with further proposals for drastic measures against the unemployed. These, then, were the bitter fruits of the National 'alliance' which the unemployed movement, for all its efforts, had been unable to destroy.

A Movement Imprisoned

The 1932 march had brought a high level of police activity in terms of spying and arrests, as well as violence. Documentation recently 'lost' by the Keeper of the Public Records shows that the South Walian Communist Bill Paynter, fined £5 for 'wilfully obstructing' the police, was the subject of an effort by the Assistant Commissioner to link him with a van allegedly containing weapons.[71] Regular reports were being filed by local police spies on all of the local leaders, with the clear purpose of anticipating the plans of the marchers, and of bringing out evidence which could be used either in trials, or in political statements denigrating march leaders.

The result was that, soon after the end of the 1932 march, the bulk of the national leadership of the NUWM was imprisoned. Hannington was taken out at a crucial point in an NAC meeting, tried and given three months for 'inciting the police' after an unsuccessful attempt at framing him. Elias, recently returned from Moscow, was given two years soon afterwards for supposedly 'attempting to cause discontent and disaffection' by virtue of letters he wrote to Hannington from the Soviet Union. Five days after the Elias trial had ended, Emhrys Llewellyn and Tom Mann were both tried for sedition, and chose prison instead of fines. The imprisonments went beyond the NUWM itself: Kay Beauchamp and Bessie Leigh of the Communist Party were imprisoned because the *Daily Worker* printed a resolution in support of Elias. Arthur Horner, who had previously held office in the NUWM, could not help because he was already in jail serving fifteen months for trying to prevent an eviction in South Wales.[72] Harry McShane was the only major national leader who had not been jailed; it was not the case, as he wrote in his autobiography, that Mann and Llewellyn were 'let off'.[73] Here was a serious situation indeed: whilst the leaders of the unemployed languished in jail, the NUWM was compelled by the duties of solidarity to spend much of its time in campaigns to release them, instead of strengthening its work on the ground.

NUWM militants, when offered the possibility of paying fines, or of being bound over, invariably refused these options and chose prison. In doing so they followed the policy of many before and since who have shown their defiance of the courts and asserted their right to protest. Once in prison they continued their resistance. That beacon of socialism, Tom Mann, was imprisoned at the age of 78 and many were concerned for his well-being. One would-be benefactor offered to stand surety for him to allow him to get out to spend Christmas with his family. He replied:

> Your kindness in offering to stand as surety for me that I may have Christmas at Home is exceedingly nice, and I am real grateful for this evidence of continued friendship. I have thought it well over and am definitely of opinion that to give the undertaking called for would be a step in wrong direction, a start on the slippery slope ...[74]

The militants of the unemployed movement accepted their imprisonment, not of course in the sense that they thought it justified, but in the sense that they thought it their price that they had to pay for social progress. The law, they pointed out, had always had to be broken by early trade unionists and democrats in order to establish rights that were now enjoyed by all. Inside prison, they used the time both to discuss with fellow-prisoners and to study and develop their own ideas. Sid Elias, for example, attended prison classes in current affairs, regularly contributing to make political points to his fellow students. He later had an opportunity to study further with a job in the prison library.[75] Whenever possible the imprisoned leaders found ways of dealing with outstanding pieces of business despite prison rules. Messages proclaiming their continued allegiance to the movement and its aims were often smuggled out and published.

Prison was nevertheless a difficult experience for everyone involved, both in terms of morale and physical side-effects. In this period in jail, Mann, who was in Brixton with Hannington, made light of his constantly cold feet, but had earlier pointed out with concern the effect that the time was having on his comrade: 'I think he too looks paler than he should, I think he is liable to an occasional breakdown and ought to be medically examined at once.'[76]

The very fact of imprisonment brought sympathy and gratitude from many both inside and outside of the NUWM who recognised what was being done on their behalf. The NUWM, far more than any other labour movement organisation of this time, was seen within that movement as a persecuted group. By reacting in the way that they did, its members earned considerable respect. This respect was largely limited to those already committed to the labour movement, but there was also a tendency among those middle-class people interested in civil liberties to see the NUWM leaders as victims of blatant repression and an alliance between sections of the intelligentsia, the NUWM and the Communist Party was starting to take shape at this time. One of the most positive outcomes of the 1932 Hunger March was the stimulus that police harassment gave to the foundation of the (National) Council for Civil Liberties, whose work continues to this day.[77] But the generation of a coalition between the NUWM and a stratum of intellectuals was a price that the government could afford to pay for its policy. The vital alliance for the NUWM was with the organisations of the employed working class, which could exert power at the point of production. This alliance was as far away as ever, largely because the depths of the Depression brought enormous fear to employed people. But it has also to be recognised that the ideological offensive against the movement of which trials and imprisonment were a part, had confirmed some trade unionists in the view that, as one Labour councillor in the 1920s had put it, the unemployed movement was 'not respectable'.[78] The images of criminality and the old fears of the 'mob' which were conjured up by the government's policy had their effect. They imposed real limitations on the size and influence of the NUWM at a time when the movement was in the midst of some of its most impressive mobilisations. It was in this sense, as well as the literal one, that the leaders of the NUWM were imprisoned.

Notes

1 Mitchell and Deane, op.cit., p.66.
2 *Manchester Guardian*, 24 September 1930.
3 Ibid., 30 November 1936.
4 Mitchell and Deane, op.cit., p.345.
5 *The Worker*, 29 August 1930.
6 NAC *Report* 23-24 August 1930, p.8.
7 *The Worker*, 29 August 1930.
8 Ibid., 10 October 1930.
9 *Report* of the Seventh Annual Conference, 21-23 February 1931, p.5.
10 *The Worker*, 3 January 1931.
11 E.H. Carr, *The Twilight of Comintern*, London 1982, p.208.
12 Interview with Phil Abrahams by Hywel Francis (South Wales Miners' Library) quoted in H. Francis, *Miners Against Fascism, Wales and the Spanish Civil War*, London 1984, p.50.
13 *The Worker*, 3 January 1931.
14 Kingsford, op.cit., pp.124-5; Bruley, op.cit., p.222.
15 *The Worker*, April 18 1930.
16 Ibid., 6 January 1931.
17 NUWM *Constitution and Rules* (n.d.,green) (WH/CP/A3a).
18 'Advice to Branches on the Defence of Claims' (n.d.) (WH/CP/A3b).
19 NAC *Report*, 7-8 May 1932, p.6.
20 Ibid.
21 *Daily Worker*, 28 January 1930.
22 *The Worker*, 25 July 1930.
23 Hughes of Kidgrove to Legal Department, 29 July 1939 (WH/MML/A.VII.IB).
24 Ibid.
25 NAC *Report*, 11-12 July 1931.
26 *Party Organiser*, No.8, December 1932, p.36.
27 *Report* of the Seventh Annual Conference, p.3.
28 W. Hannington, *Ten Lean Years*, London 1940, pp.38-49.
29 Eddie Jones, Item 15, South Wales Coalfield Archive.
30 *The Worker*, 3 October 1931.
31 M.Cohen, *I Was One of the Unemployed*, London 1945, pp.17-27. Despite Cohen's reference to the Unemployment Act, a more explicit passage on p.20 suggests that this demonstration was held in 1931.
32 W. Gray, M. Jenkins, E. and R. Frow, *Unemployed Demonstrations Salford and Manchester 1931*, Manchester 1981, pp.4-9.
33 *Manchester Guardian*, quoted in Ibid., p.10.

34 Ibid., p.12.
35 J.M.Bellamy and J.Saville (eds), *Dictionary of Labour Biography*, London 1977, Vol.4, p.80.
36 *The Times*, 3,5,6,9,15 October 1931.
37 *The Worker*, 28 November 1931.
38 R. Hayburn, 'The Response to Unemployment in the 1930s, with particular Reference to South-East Lancashire', unpublished PhD Thesis, University of Hull, 1970, pp.483-4.
39 *The Worker*, 5 December 1931.
40 J. Attfield and S. Williams (eds), *1939. The Communist Party and the War*, London 1984, pp.94-6.
41 NAC *Report*, 17-18 September 1932, p.1.
42 *The Worker*, 20,27 June, 11 July 1931.
43 Hayburn, op.cit., pp.622-3.
44 *The Worker*, 3 January 1931; *Weekly Worker*, 30 January, 23 April, 4 June 1932.
45 *The Worker*, 19 December 1931.
46 *Weekly Worker*, 4 June 1932.
47 NAC *Report*, 7-8 May 1932, pp.12-3.
48 Ibid.
49 *Weekly Worker*, 16 July 1932.
50 Ibid., 30 July 1932.
51 *Unemployed Special*, October 1932.
52 NAC *Report on Demonstrations on National Day of Struggle* (WH/MML), p.1.
53 NAC *Report*, 7-8 May 1932.
54 *Unemployed Special*, No.3.
55 NAC *Report*, 25 February 1933.
56 *Unemployed Leader*, August 1934.
57 *The Unemployed Demonstrator,* n.d. (WH/MML).
58 NAC *Report*, 17-18 September 1932, pp.2-5.
59 Ibid., p.7.
60 Interview with John Jackson, 4 July 1983.
61 Hannington, *Ten Lean Years*, pp.60-5; P. Devlin, *Yes, We Have No Bananas,* Belfast 1981, p.122.
62 Interview with Jack McGougan, 15 August 1985.
63 *Ten Lean Years*, pp.60-5.
64 NAC *Report*, 3-4 December 1932.
65 The phrase is that of the *Irish Workers Voice*, 15 October 1932, quoted by R. Munck and B. Rolston in 'Belfast in the 1930s: An Oral History Project', *Oral History*, Vol.12, No.1, p.15. Munck and Rolston take issue with Paddy Devlin's *Yes, We Have No Bananas*.
66 Devlin, op.cit., p.131.
67 McShane and Smith, op.cit., p.107.
68 Interview with Dora Cox, *Link*, No.32.
69 NAC *Report*, 3-4 December 1932.
70 Film shown in *Jerusalem's Army* (Central Television; videotape in Central TV's archive).
71 Francis and Smith, op.cit., p.106.
72 *Unemployed Struggles*, Chapter 15; *Never On Our Knees*, pp.259-79; A.

Horner, *Incorrigible Rebel*, London 1960, pp.113-9.

73 McShane and Smith, op.cit., p.193.

74 Tom Mann to Mr Marlow, 21 December 1932 (Tom Mann Archive, Coventry).

75 Interview with Sid Elias, 7 April 1984.

76 Tom Mann to Mam, 17 January 1933. (Tom Mann Archive, Coventry).

77 See Sylvia Scaffardi, *Fire Under the Carpet: Working For Civil Liberties in the 1930s*, London 1986, pp.31.-44.

78 *Barrow Guardian*, 20 October 1923.

7

The Plateau, 1933-35

By the spring of 1933, the NUWM was operating in a distinctly unfavourable international climate. Whilst the French and American unemployed movements respectively had their Hunger Marches banned and attacked, the entire German working-class movement was undergoing a much more serious attack by the Nazis. The NUWM could only look on, express its solidarity and hope that the brown plague could be kept at bay. The NAC sent fraternal greetings to the German workers faced with capitalism's 'last weapon', but already sensed that the last weapon was proving terrifyingly effective.[1] The signs in Britain were not encouraging. The National government had successfully implanted police spies throughout the movement, whilst there were absolute bans on demonstrations in many major towns. In November 1932, the Royal Commission recommended further cuts in unemployment benefit, a tightening of the Means Test and higher national insurance contributions from the employed. The NUWM faced, as Hannington later recalled, 'Grave threats of worsened conditions'.[2] Would the movement be able to respond adequately to the challenge? The situation facing those in employment who were organised was if anything even more worrying. Concern was expressed on the NAC that mass strike-breaking was becoming a reality. In the strikes which took place at Hillmans Coaches and Firestones in 1932, the employers had been able to recruit armies of scabs. It was recorded with trepidation that 'the employers are now beginning to break through our defences' because of increased poverty.[3] Did this disturbing trend presage the fascist destruction of trade unionism, and the unemployed movement with it?

The NUWM in 1933

Despite these very real concerns, the NUWM stood at an organisational highpoint in 1933. Unemployment on an unprecedented scale had provided the NUWM with a massive potential membership. By February 1933, the movement was able to claim 100,000 members organised in 349 branches, 36 District Councils and 34 women's sections.[4] The NUWM was strongest in the mining areas, particularly South Wales and Scotland, but at this point could reasonably be portrayed as a national organistion, even if in some areas (East Anglia, for example) it remained very weak. But there was still much room for growth, when only about one unemployed person in thirty adhered to the movement. The NUWM was the size of a larger trade union of the time, but its constituency was wider than that of most unions.

The level of activity however was considerably higher than in any trade union. The typical activist spent long hours representing, speaking and organising. The militants who could be best described as 'typical' were young men, miners or skilled engineers from the industrial areas, invariably with Communist or Labour Party cards. The District Councils were dominated by the CPGB, whilst this was even truer of the NAC, which had just one Labour Party member, Len Youle of Sheffield, among its number. For these people, involvement in the NUWM was a practical expression of their commitment to the wider struggle for socialism, taken up because they were out of work. Those few members who were in work but chose to support the NUWM were also generally of this type. Eddie Collins, a Yorkshire miner was such a member. Involved in the Labour Party, he had briefly been associated with the Communist Party at its foundation. All of these people were driven by a burning desire for radical social change; arguing about benefits and the like was strictly subordinate to these wider aims. Many of them spent hours each week propagandising in public about the evils of capitalism and the socialist alternative. Sharing the fate of the unemployed, they remained extremely close to their concerns.

Such were the people who formed the backbone of the NUWM at this time. The average member of the NUWM had only a fleeting association with the movement, paying only a few penny subscriptions before he or she fell out of touch, found work (very few people continued paying subs when back in work), or moved. These people tended to be young, unskilled and not afraid either of the Communist image of the movement, nor of the prospect of violence on demonstrations. Most of those joining did so to try to get better treatment from local bureaucrats, and to improve benefits, according to Sid Elias. Some ordinary members developed a more sustained commitment after finding an outlet for their talents in the NUWM, often developing politically in turn. John Jackson of Birkenhead and Mr Hudson of Bradford were representative of these people. Both joined because of a very human sense of outrage at the way the unemployed were treated, and remained involved when they felt they were doing something useful as propagandist and printer of leaflets respectively.

The membership of the NUWM remained overwhelmingly male, but the involvement of women was growing. Although not a member of the CPGB, Maud Brown had, since her appointment as national women's organiser, made the NUWM the principal focus of Communist women's agitational activity. But it was the government itself, with its Anomalies Regulations issued in late 1932, that provided the main motive for women to join the NUWM. These regulations led to a high rate of refusal of benefit to women and caused tremendous resentment as thousands of women were struck off the unemployed register. The women were offered domestic service, but this was not regarded as acceptable by the majority of them. The 1932 Hunger March's women's contingent, which chanted 'Work, work, work, we want to work' on its way, did not have domestic service in mind, nor did anyone except Labour Exchange officials. The Hunger March increased the number of women's sections quite rapidly from about a dozen to 34 by early 1933.[5]

The influx of new members revitalised many branches. In February 1933, *Unemployed Leader* carried an article by Joe Smith, the secretary of the Northampton branch of the NUWM, which described the development of the local organisation from an unemployed association into a 'powerful, militant organisation' during 1932. An initial meeting with Tom Mann (the starting point for many branches), the creation of a 'very broad united front reception committee' for the Hunger Marchers, and a successful campaign for increased winter relief brought in 450 new members. Smith claimed a prodigious level of activity for the branch. During 1932, 325 outdoor and 51 indoor meetings had been held, 27 demonstrations and deputations had been organised, 26 cases defended at the Court of Referees and many campaigns conducted. In the mining areas, branches were often quite large and well housed in relation to the towns in which they operated. The Shirebrook branch in Derbyshire boasted 600 members and a hut as a base which had been donated by Billy Green, a local Communist. This was a considerable presence in a small town.[6]

Several branches performed considerable feats in the 1930s in terms of building their own premises. The Gorseinon branch in South Wales completed its own branch headquarters by 1935. Some of these local headquarters were quite impressive; the Kirkcaldy branch had what was described as a 'fine bookshop and club' attached to theirs. The tremendous enterprise shown by branches in developing such valuable resources surely paid off in terms of providing an important focus for organisation. With their shelter and facilities these places attracted the unemployed, and created opportunities for social contact. The NUWM was providing a service which in turn helped it to build its relationship with the unemployed.[7]

The NUWM, for all its strength and national organisation, nevertheless still had to recognise that in many areas there were in existence local unemployed associations. The majority of these had a different (usually Labour Party) political outlook, but there were also a few that had fallen out with the NUWM national leadership. An example of the first type of association was that in Bury St Edmunds, where George Freezer, a Labour Party member, organised a committee which held meetings and ran Christmas parties for the children of the unemployed. Its style was non-militant, and Freezer was careful not to upset local dignitaries, but still identified sufficiently with Wal Hannington to ask him to speak locally.[8] An example of the second type was Bradford, where Harry Goldthorpe led the branch out of the NUWM in 1932. The immediate cause was a visit from Lily Webb, a dedicated Communist organiser long active in the unemployed movement. Mr Hudson, of Bradford, recalled:

The day that she arrived, it was a clash of personalities really. Goldthorpe was present and I remember Lily Webb ... and it was just a gesture of hers, typical of the party members of the day: 'Comrade, here!' And of course, Goldthorpe, 'er ... what's this, like?' This beckoning, I could see from his expression he didn't like this and they got into some discussion and the net result was that there was a real argy-bargy between them, and he just as much as told them not to come any more.[9]

The 'Goldthorpe mob', as they became known, retained the formal statements of the objects of the NUWM, and there was no official split, but headquarters directives carried no weight in Bradford. The 'mob' set up in a disused warehouse in Quebec Street, converting the attic into a chicken run which provided the canteen with eggs, bringing in two billiards tables and using the ground floor as a sewing machine shop. Money was raised by concerts and dances, and coal and food distributed to the unemployed. This co-existed with some militant demonstrating and representation.[10]

Both Bury St Edmunds-style moderacy and Bradford-style rebellions were symptoms of a strong feeling for local autonomy which existed within many NUWM branches, and which was rooted in a 'self-help' philosophy. 'Self-help' children's parties and chicken runs were clearly best organised on a local level, and required no help from the national body. This persistent feeling of localism worried the national leadership more than ever in the early 1930s, simply because the expansion of the movement made it more apparent, and because the period was one in which fierce attacks on the unemployed nationally made the leaders increasingly anxious to develop an adequate national response. Headquarters therefore redoubled its efforts to strengthen allegiance to the national movement and its perspective of unremitting struggle. It pursued this aim by increasing its office resources and deluging the branches with a series of circulars and directives, by appointing 'national propagandists' who worked from the office for short periods whenever funds permitted, by making regular appeals for funds to branches and by other initiatives. One such initiative was the attempt to create a National Activities Brigade during 1933. The members of this Brigade (the military reference is typical) were to co-ordinate local responses to headquarters campaigns. But the problem overwhelmed its putative solution: just twenty-seven volunteers were attracted.[11]

The thrust of headquarters policy was not a complete failure, as the increasing size and discipline of Hunger Marches witnesses. Yet many problems remained in terms of the ability of London headquarters to launch co-ordinated campaigns behind specific demands, as circulars to branches regularly complained. Allegiance to national figures, especially Wal Hannington, ('Mr NUWM' as one old militant described him) was not sufficiently translated into action on their circulars.[12] Moreoever, there was a price to be paid for the efforts to make the NUWM a more centralised body. Some of these have already been mentioned, but in 1933 the most obvious consequences occurred in terms of the NUWM's ability to bring in more local unemployed associations to their own ranks. In a period in which the Communist-dominated NAC still had a relatively hostile attitude to the Labour Party and all its works, decisions were taken to actively exclude some types of Labour Party support. The refusal to accept Labour MPs as sponsors of the 1932 Hunger March was a case in point. At a local level this had an effect on the way that unemployed associations, often dominated by Labour Party members, saw the NUWM. In a disciplined NUWM, such people might have asked themselves if there was room for Labour Party supporters in the movement. The government and the TUC both sensed the possibility of building an alternative to the NUWM.

The Launch of a New Government Initiative for the Unemployed

One of Hannington's very real qualities was his ability to perceive governmental strategies at an early stage. During his time in prison, he had been told by the prison chaplain that the Hunger March had not been entirely futile, because it had stimulated the government to find 'real' alternatives to agitation. The National government, just after the departure of the first marchers from home, launched a campaign for the development of local centres for the unemployed. The Prime Minister and the Prince of Wales broadcast appeals to the nation to help in raising funds and providing equipment for recreational centres for the workless. Government funds were made available to the National Council of Social Service and the Quakers for helping the unemployed to obtain and cultivate allotments. Hannington saw the new centres as a dual threat: to the NUWM, because the unemployed would be drawn into recreational activities rather than protest, and to the employed, whose terms and conditions of employment would be undermined when the centres did productive work which ought to be paid at trade union rates.[13]

Hannington fully grasped the threat posed by these schemes, and realised how important it was to make out the arguments as fully as possible to the widest audience, when confronted by this major state drive. The BBC had played an important part in the government's publicity, whilst its journal the *Listener* opened its columns to discussion on how the scheme could be improved. In January 1933, the Prince of Wales came to the microphone to introduce a series of talks dealing with the position of the unemployed. Hannington therefore wrote to J.H.Whitley, Chairman of the BBC's Board of Governors, asking for the opportunity to broadcast in the series. His request was turned down on the grounds that the talks were based on the experience of the unemployed themselves, and that the Corporation wished to avoid political controversy. In other words, remarked the *Daily Worker*, the BBC only wanted the 'non-controversial' voice of the capitalist class to be heard. The NUWM was not prepared to accept these 'explanations', and a deputation went to Broadcasting House, where they were met by two detectives and a member of the BBC management who agreed to pass on their request to be heard. They were invited to return by Charles Siepmann, the Director of Talks, and when the deputation returned with Hannington at its head, there was a full police guard surrounding the building. In an interview in which establishment liberalism was confronted by Communist indignation for an hour and a half, the delegation grew increasingly frustrated. The NUWM request was again rejected. In a press statement, the NUWM said that by its decision the BBC had placed itself in politics as a strong supporter of the National government and of die-hard starvation policies. The NUWM promised a strong protest from the working-class movement as a whole.[14]

The BBC had argued that the talks in question, entitled 'SOS' and conducted by S.P.B. Mais, were not political, but reports of their content in the *Listener* show conclusively that the NUWM had been right to protest. For example, when Mais reported that he had attended a meeting of unemployed people in Lincoln to discuss the formation of clubs for the workless, a 'black-haired youth' stood up and asked:

> How anyone could expect an unemployed man to do physical jerks on 15s. a week, or play ping-pong while his wife was sitting at home before a half-empty grate with only margarine to eat.

Mais stayed on after the meeting to talk to this young man, who proved resistant to his point of view:

> He wouldn't allow that these clubs were doing any good at all. 'They're only meant', he said, 'to keep us quiet by people who are afraid.' He was right of course in suggesting that ping-pong does not provide a final solution. But he was wrong in denying that the service does no good at all.[15]

Since the NUWM alternative of active protest was passed over in silence, Mais was clearly propagandising for the National Council for Social Service. The BBC could not, or would not, see that this was a political issue. The NUWM protest had in this case been rejected, but its opposition had not been entirely without effect in the medium term. The next series to deal with the unemployment issue, broadcast during the winter of 1933-34, relied much more heavily on the reflections of the unemployed themselves. The result was that protests showed through as they spoke. Public awareness was being raised in a way which the Prime Minister did not like, and MacDonald tried to stop the series in its tracks. The NUWM was at least partly responsible for creating the political climate within which it was felt by the BBC that the voices of the unemployed, speaking directly, ought to be heard.[16]

The fact remained that the NCSS centres had been launched, and middle-class volunteers were brought in by the publicity. The NCSS centres, as they developed with the help of government money, were a real problem for a labour movement whose influence had been greatly weakened by the

Depression. It was in this context, with existing conditions of employment threatened by the new scheme, that the TUC decided to make another attempt to organise the unemployed. The NUWM, with its militant, campaigning style, was now confronted by two major rivals with quite different views on what ought to be done for the unemployed.

The TUC's Revived Unemployed Associations

In January 1932 the TUC General Council decided to make another attempt at establishing unemployed associations under the control of Trades Councils, and in February sent two delegates to an important meeting in Bristol, called by the city's Unemployed Association to discuss the co-ordination of unemployed associations on a national basis. There was a large demonstration outside the Conference, fuelled by resentment at the Bristol Unemployed Association's refusal to support an NUWM demonstration earlier in the month which had ended in fighting with the police. There was also considerable dissension inside the Conference hall. 30 unemployed associations were represented (although *Weekly Worker* claimed that twelve of these were no more than paper organisations). A number of those present were either members, or sympathisers of the NUWM, and the TUC position of having a federation under the control of Trades Councils was defeated. The TUC delegates therefore had to announce that they would wash their hands of any federation that was set up. Although the decision was taken to set up a National Federation of Unemployed Associations, this was less damaging to the NUWM than it was to the TUC, which had no way of influencing the new body. Once again, the NUWM had succeeded in splitting the TUC from some of its potential supporters.[17]

Despite this setback, the TUC Conference accepted the General Council's proposals in September 1932. Several years of vituperative criticism of the TUC 'bureaucrats' had driven many delegates away from the NUWM and convinced them of the need for an alternative. The General Council submitted Model Rules for associations, under which all business was to be transacted through the appropriate Trades Council, which would control their accounts. The association could speak at

the Trades Councils, but only on unemployment-related
issues. This was the distinctly unpromising basis on which the
TUC proposed to do battle with the NUWM and the
government-funded National Council for Social Service
centres.

Soon after the TUC's decision to set up unemployed
associations, Hannington published a short pamphlet, *Crimes
Against the Unemployed*, which he subtitled 'An Exposure of the
TUC Scab Scheme and the Crimes Committed Against the
Unemployed by the General Council'. The pamphlet argued
that the associations would be 'Cinderellas' because they were
purely local and under the influence of Trades Councils. It
was boldly predicted that: 'Our movement will break through
the lines of the scabs wherever they dare to show themselves.'[19]
Meanwhile, Emryhs Llewellyn was condemning the TUC for
co-operating with the National Playing Fields Association to
provide games facilities for the associations, denouncing this
as being similar to the government idea of drilling the
unemployed into 'healthy cannon fodder, and to infuse into
them a spirit of fascism'.[20] These were strong words, intended
to alert the movement's membership to the seriousness of the
new threat.

In several cases, the NUWM and the Communist Party
succeeded in nipping associations in the bud on Trades
Councils. In Barrow, the Executive of the Trades Council
recommended support for the scheme, but were overturned by
a wrecking amendment in full Council; in Plymouth,
left-wingers defeated the motion outright.[21] By 1935, a TUC
survey revealed that 52 Trades Councils had unemployed
associations, with a membership of 22,420. The General
Council asserted that this was only half the number that
actually existed. Even if the General Council's claim is
accepted, this would mean that the associations had less than
half of the membership of the NUWM at that time. But the
geographical distribution of the associations also has to be
taken into account. By late 1933, after a year's effort, there
were only two associations in Scotland.[22] Elsewhere, the
associations were strongest in Lancashire, Cheshire and
North Wales, Yorkshire and the South Wales coalfield.[23] In
1939 the Trades Council Conference passed a resolution
asking for full-time support for the associations, and this

would no doubt have improved the TUC's prospects of
realising the success that they habitually claimed in their
reports.[24] During the 1930s, the associations, accurately
described by Hannington as small social clubs, were often
fertile soil for the NUWM to implant itself.

The Regional Marches of 1933

Hannington warned persistently during 1933 that the political
situation was very threatening to the unemployed. With the
unemployed movement's very existence being put in question,
the National government was, he warned, preparing further
attacks. Hannington and the NAC decided that the only
appropriate response to the situation was massive mobilisation. With the relief system having been restructured
around the regional PACs, they adopted a strategy of regional
marches, which would have the dual advantage of striking
where the opposition was as yet ill prepared, and of
maximising local participation. On this foundation, the
ground could be prepared for a major national Hunger
March.

Considering the importance of this strategy there have been
few and sparse accounts of these marches; this may have been
in part because Hannington did not have direct personal
experience of them, and did not therefore deal with them
extensively in his own writings. But the extent of these
marches is very impressive. At the end of February, the NAC
heard that one successful regional march, to Durham, had
been held already, and that similar marches were being held
in Fife and Lanarkshire that weekend. In June, a march to
Edinburgh was organised, contemporaneously with marches
to Preston and Wakefield. By the late summer, regional
marches were planned for Cornwall, Kent, Northumberland,
Derbyshire, Monmouthshire, Lancashire, Glamorgan,
Aberdeenshire, Fife, Ayrshire, Dumbartonshire, Lanarkshire,
Renfrewshire and Glasgow. The movement was literally an
organisation on the march in 1933.[25]

The summer marches to Edinburgh and Preston were both
the subject of pamphlets written by their leaders, Harry
McShane and Phil Harker respectively. McShane's pamphlet
is interesting for the politics of its account. Given the

self-consciously 'Bolshevik' title *Three Days That Shook Edinburgh*, it triumphantly announced 'a signal and historic triumph for the United Front'. The Scottish march of several hundreds from Glasgow to Edinburgh had certainly awoken parts of the population of Edinburgh to the problems of the industrial areas. The young unemployed, including many women, had joined with the marchers to parade through the Royal Palace of Holyrood playing Connolly's 'Rebel Song' and 'The Internationale', had forced the authorities to give them the Oddfellows Hall to sleep in for several nights, and had held numerous meetings. The marchers had demanded to see Sir Godfrey Collins, the Secretary of State for Scotland, to put their demands, but failed in this. In the end, there was a battle with the authorities over the marchers' wish for free transport home. The Chief Constable and Town Clerk deputy told McShane that they required a guarantee that there would be no more marches to Edinburgh in return for the transport. McShane refused to give such an undertaking, and the Chief Constable, worried about law and order in Edinburgh if he did not concede, gave in. McShane's pamphlet, in typical NUWM style for the period, ringingly announced: 'The working class had broken through! A smashing victory had been obtained!'[26] Nevertheless, Sir Godfrey Collins had not appeared.

The Edinburgh march, if it did not quite justify the assessment put on it by its leader, was still a success in certain respects. The movement in Scotland had maintained its momentum during the usually slack summer period, and had gained considerable publicity for its activities as well as a free trip home. The Lancashire march was slightly more successful, since it had the more tangible result of forcing the PAC to agree that claimants who were aggrieved because of their treatment locally should have the right of appeal to it.[27]

Hannington expressed himself in slightly less triumphalist terms than McShane and Harker, but nevertheless insisted that the regional marches were important. He argued that they caused 'considerable hesitancy' within the government, which was waiting to introduce a new and damaging Unemployment Bill based on the Report of the Royal Commission.[28] At the Eighth National Conference held in Manchester in April 1933, Hannington had warned that it

would not be long before such measures were taken. The
movement's marches had played a part in putting off this evil
hour, but the new Bill was published before the year was out.

The 1934 Hunger March

Hannington had predicted before the Bill was published that
its main thrust would be to reduce benefit rates and to bring in
'industrial centres' to create a 'new slave class' which would
form the basis of fascism in Britain. In the event, his central
predictions were correct. In outline, the Bill proposed to
stabilise the level of benefits first established as 'temporary' in
1931; the retention of the Means Test together with
expanded grounds for disqualification, and the administration
of 'transitional' payments by a new body, the Unemployed
Assistance Board. In addition, the payment of transitional
benefit was to be made dependent on attendance at training
centres. This attendance was a part of a wider strategy,
Hannington insisted, of creating a large pool of cheap labour
to undercut the position of the employed working class. It had
to be seen as a plan to emulate the extensive schemes of
voluntary labour set up in Germany, which had so impressed
the Royal Commission. Because relief work was too costly as
far as the state was concerned, the unemployed were to be
forced to attend either training centres or NCSS centres.
There they could become accustomed to the idea of working
for nothing. A leaf was being taken out of Hitler's book.[29]
Taken as a whole, the government measures constituted a
grave threat to the whole working-class movement.

This analysis was broadly accepted by the Communist
Party, which strongly advocated a wide and non-sectarian
response from the labour movement. An appeal was sent out
by leading members of the CPGB, ILP and some leading trade
unionists for a 'Congress of Action' to be held in December
1933. This 'United Front Committee' included Jack Tanner of
the important Amalgamated Engineering Union, the first
major trade union leader to associate himself with a
Communist or NUWM initiative for some years. The
committee suggested to the NUWM a Hunger March, to
precede the Congress. The leading Communist Willie
Gallacher argued to the NAC of the NUWM that a Hunger

March was vitally important for the purpose of building a United Front. Hannington and McShane opposed the plan on the grounds that Hunger Marches required adequate preparation, and, particularly, that further support should be requested from the trade union movement. But such was the influence of the new emphasis on a 'united front' within the Communist Party that the party's position was carried at the NAC. Unusually, and revealingly, the Communist Party had been able to oppose the combined weight of Hannington and McShane and carry the NAC with it. Preparations for the march began immediately.[30] The 1934 Hunger March involved at least 700 people from beginning to end, was well supported by the trade union and labour movements in comparison to its immediate predecessors, and experienced very little violence at any stage. On this occasion, influenced by the growing tendency within the Communist Party to look for alliances with Labour politicians, the NUWM accepted the support of Labour MPs. The marchers' petition was presented at the bar of the House by Jack McGovern, one of the famous group of Clydeside left-wing MPs. There was some small irony in this, for McGovern had been specifically singled out for very hostile criticism from both Hannington and McShane in 1932 as a 'reactionary' for having said that the NUWM obviously had not wanted its petition presented at the bar of the House of Commons. McGovern, Hannington said, had only wanted to get on the NUWM bandwagon in 1932. In 1934, he was invited onto it.[31]

The unemployed movement had clearly changed its attitude to the 'left' Labour MPs over the previous two years. Far more attention was now being paid to persuading MPs in general. On 22 February 1934, Harry McShane and Lewis Jones had addressed a meeting of MPs at Westminster. The two NUWM leaders, said a headquarters circular, had made 'a profound impression'. Not one of the MPs could destroy their case. The circular went on to claim that the government was 'on the run', and was 'shaken'.[32] It is quite possible that men of the intellectual power of McShane and Jones had impressed the MPs whom they had addressed, and had made a small contribution to the success of the march in this way. The only pity was that they had been prevented by Communist Party policy from doing so earlier.

The 1934 march had been notable for its 'iron discipline' internally and its wide support externally. There were some problems, but these were not always of the type that have been portrayed in the leaders' accounts, of marchers stealing from other marchers and having to be expelled, and so on. The South Coast contingent, for example, at one point demanded a day's rest from marching and meeting in London, a suggestion that did not meet with the approval of the march leaders.[33] The high level of discipline may well have been one of the reasons for the lack of violence on the march, which may in turn have helped it to gain wide support. The national Congress held after the march was certainly very broadly-based, with nearly 1,500 delegates, including some trade union and Labour Party figures. Hannington was justified when he later called it a historic development in terms of bringing together such people.[34] The new found unity was useful to Harry Pollitt and Tom Mann, who were both arrested in South Wales for making 'seditious' speeches. Twenty lodges of the South Wales Miners' Federation, as well as numerous other trade union bodies, made contributions to their defence fund.[35] More importantly, the movement won an important concession for the unemployed just one month after the end of the march. The Chancellor announced that the 10 per cent cuts of 1931 were to be restored from July. The NUWM could claim a major step forward, even though the Unemployment Bill was still hanging over their heads.

Police Spies and the 1934 March

One of the reasons for the 'iron discipline' on the 1934 march was the fear of the NUWM leadership that police spies were operating within the movement. It seems unlikely, however, that they fully grasped the extent of police information on the NUWM, which was quite extensive. The police seem to have shifted, possibly under the force of middle-class pressure after 1932, away from a policy of 'stick' towards the NUWM, and towards a policy of intensive information-gathering. By 1934, the Metropolitan Police under Lord Trenchard (sometimes dubbed a 'fascist' by the Communist Party) certainly had been discouraged from appearing too sympathetic to the unemployed. Trenchard insisted that whereas in the past the police had sometimes held concerts and given the proceeds to the unemployed,

> That sort of thing must not go on in the Hunger March, though it was a very good trait in the police to want to help the unemployed. It would, however, probably lead to statements in the press that the Commissioner of Police had issued an order to help the Marchers![36]

By the time of the 1934 march, the police had an informer on the NAC, or at least someone very close to a member of the national leadership.[37] Special Branch reports, often very detailed, were also available on local figures within the movement. The information gathered was used to help in developing cases against individuals, or, as in the case of Bill Paynter in 1934, to try to connect people with certain events. The leaders of the movement were aware of the level of police interest in them; in fact, it had been impossible to ignore since 1932 when policemen were found asleep in the doorways of houses in which NAC members had stayed overnight in London![38] They also knew that the police were tapping their telephones.[39]

The type of security required to deal with these levels of police interest had an adverse effect on the democratic process within the unemployed movement. There were occasions noted by the police themselves when meetings being addressed by leading members on the NUWM were asked to take certain statements on trust, and not to question them.[40] Internal documents had to be written with a police readership in mind. This may have been one of the reasons for the NAC not reporting reasons for the expulsion of members during the 1930s. It was unnerving for the members of the NAC to suspect, as they did, that one of their number was a police informer. But above all, it was difficult to maintain the fullest internal democracy under such conditions.

Against the 'Slave Mentality'

The Unemployment Insurance Bill received the Royal assent on 28 June 1934. The first part of the Bill dealt with the proposed expansion of Ministry of Labour training camps. It was now to become a statutory requirement for anyone claiming insurance benefit to attend a training camp if required to do so by the national insurance officer. Previously, this power had only existed in the case of claimants under the age of eighteen. The Communist Party saw this as another step down the British road to fascism. The camps became symbolic of a broader growth of compulsion, repression and legalised Nazism, and not just as another measure against the unemployed. The background to this feeling was of course being painted in Germany as the Nazis imprisoned, interned, tortured and murdered Communists and trade unionists. Hannington, with his German connections and association with the various Communist international aid networks developed in the 1920s, was particularly conscious of these developments. It was no wonder, then, that he described the 'Slave Concentration Camps' as the most serious attack in the legislation.[41] Here was proof positive, the Communists felt, that the National government wanted to smash the organised working class, and to encourage the 'slave mentality' that would prepare the way for war against the Soviet Union. This was the vision that they conjured up within the unemployed movement.

The government argued that the new camps were not related to the separate injection of funds into the National Council of Social Services (NCSS) centres. Hannington and the NUWM consistently asserted that this was untrue, explaining that the NCSS centres had initally been presented as recreational, but had then become work-oriented. The two schemes were seen as part of the same overall plan with the aim of totally degrading labour and introducing fascism by degrees. It was a problem for those in work as much as for the unemployed, Hannington argued, and in this context it was tragic that the NCSS schemes had attracted support from trade union branches. He rejected the argument that any of these plans were counter-acting the corrosive effects of idleness. The real enemy, as a local NUWM paper said, was political passivity, and in this sense all government-funded schemes actually created demoralisation. But the new legislation also introduced the element of taking people away from their homes and putting them in isolated areas for weeks on end. Many people had no wish at all to go along with these plans, and were willing to resist. The potential for building a 'United Front' of those in and out of work was considerable.[42]

By 1937, there were twenty Ministry of Labour
'Instructional Centres'. Between 1929 and 1938, just under
190,000 men passed through these centres, the peak year
being 1934 when nearly 33,000 attended. Most of the
government effort in persuading people to attend was in the
depressed areas, where the NUWM was strongest. Since the
position was always (formally speaking, at least) that
attendance was 'voluntary' even though benefit might be
refused, the NUWM also directed its main effort at getting
people to refuse to go, and then pursuing their benefit claim.
Hannington claimed that there had been some success in
developing this 'boycott spirit', and said that in the five
months ending January 1936 although over 64,000 men were
approached to attend in the 'Special' (depressed) areas, not
more than three thousand accepted.[43] The movement argued
consistently for mass refusals, and held meetings at which
letters of 'invitation' to attend were publicly burned. The
NUWM often had to fight benefit cases afterwards. The
Nottingham branch forced the PAC to pay relief in a number
of such cases, while the St Pancras branch fought a long battle
in support of a man called Cartwright who refused to go to the
long-established Hollesley Bay 'colony'. They successfully
used the opposition of the London Trades Council to all such
camps to pressurise local Labour councillors to oppose
compulsion, and the man's case was won.[44] The tenacity
shown by the branches, and the general propaganda effort,
combined to produce the striking rate of refusal in the
depressed areas which Hannington referred to.

The movement also tried to agitate inside the camps. This
was difficult because those who attended could be seen as part
of a defeated minority who agreed to attend in the first place.
In an interview with William Heard, an ex-inmate of Shobdon
camp, near Hereford, published by Dave Colledge and John
Field, the impression is of 'no sense of "community", of
solidarity, of comradeship, simply a harsh struggle to
survive'.[45] Many people clearly saw their stay in the camps as
'lost time', something to be endured. The NUWM was not
without success in organising in some camps, however.
During 1932, there was considerable NUWM activity around
the Belmont 'colony', which resulted in a group of inmates
striking work and joining the 1932 Hunger March rally in

Hyde Park. They were greeted, the *Weekly Worker* reported, by a 'thunderous roar of applause'.[46] But most of the camps were more isolated than Belmont, which was west of London. Much of the activity was focused on NUWM branches outside the camps. In Wolverhampton, Bilboe, an NUWM activist and Labour councillor, was arrested during protests at the conditions inside the camp. Sentenced to three months' imprisonment, men at the centre paid money to give to Bilboe's family.[47] In West Wales, the NUWM District Council called a demonstration on Budget Day in 1935, making a special effort to get some men from the local Brechfa camp out; seventy men joined their demonstration, in the distinctive corduroys and high boots. Afterwards, a petition was started to send the men home without loss of benefit.[48] In the summer of 1938, there was a mass walk-out at Brechfa, against the bad food, damp bedding, lack of medical supplies, semi-military discipline and the fact that men forfeited eightpence per day of their allowance if they were sick.[49] In the late 1930s, Hannington even succeeded in getting into a camp by saying he was 'from the TUC', and held a 'smashing' meeting with the men outside the fence.[50] Yet, despite the efforts of the movement to organise the inmates (a headquarters circular suggested that they should not pay subs whilst in the camp, for example), the camps remained largely unorganised in NUWM terms. Sporadic protests were perhaps all that was possible in the circumstances. But this was not in any case the main strand in the movement's response to the camps, which was the 'boycott spirit'.

An Answer to the NCSS Centres: A More Developed Social Life

The NCSS centres constituted a much more developed network than the 'slave camps'. By May 1934, the NCSS estimated that about 250,000 people were using their 2,300 clubs.[51] The clubs varied enormously, but tended to provide facilities for boot-repairing, card-playing and educational activity. The general significance of the their work lay in providing people with an opportunity for social contact.[52]

The NUWM leadership, which had not paid great attention

to developing the social side of the movement in the 1920s, started to place much greater emphasis on this during 1933 and 1934. It was suggested that trade union branches should be approached to help raise funds to provide whist drives, concerts, socials, study circles, bands, sports teams and so on. Sometimes the Communist leaders' requirements struck a faintly ludicrous note; dangers of reactionary deviations could sometimes be detected in bands, and 'care must be taken to see that these bands are kept strictly under the control of the branch'.[53] Whilst the NAC was mainly concerned with combating the influence of the NCSS centres, and with keeping control, the branches themselves often organised large-scale social events without worrying over much about their political direction. Rambles across the countryside were organised, football teams set up and large children's parties arranged. Some branches launched truly massive efforts for the children: in the late summer of 1934, for example, the Greenock branch opened a fund for a children's outing to which over £100 was subscribed. No less than 4,700 children were taken to Battery Park for a day out, given half a pint of milk and a bag of buns when they arrived, and an orange and a bag of toffee when they left. What happened in between is thankfully unrecorded. This outing then became an annual event, supported by many trade union branches and apparently greatly enjoyed by the children themselves.

At the same time, large-scale national recreational events under firm political control were also organised. In August 1934, for example, the National Congress and March Council ran a summer camp at Eastchurch on the Isle of Sheppey. The campers elected a 'Camp Control Council' which reported on arrangements to a full meeting each day. On Wednesday, when the campers signed on at Sheerness Labour Exchange, their walk took the form of a ramble which culminated in the comrades forming up in columns and marching along the promenade shouting slogans against the National government. On the Saturday, they ran a public meeting. At the end of the holiday, they elected a committee of fifteen to plan further events in conjunction with the London District Council.[54] The following year an impressive camp was run by the Oxford Trades Council and Labour Party, the South Wales Miners' Federation (SWMF) and the London District

Council of the NUWM. Every week, 50 miners all nominated by their SWMF lodges, 50 unemployed from London NUWM branches and some students attended. During the four weeks for which the camp was run, some six hundred people passed through. Each large tent elected a representative to a camp committee, which met every day to plan activities, discussed complaints and reported to a general meeting. Regular educational meetings on labour movement topics were organised, and an impressive array of speakers came to address the campers: Arthur Horner, Sid Elias, the local Communist leader Bill 'Firestone' Lazarus and G.D.H.Cole the Oxford socialist intellectual amongst them. *Unemployed Leader* took great care to point out that the holiday was under the real democratic control of those who came, unlike the social service camp at Eynsham, not far away from the NUWM's Clifton Hampden site, where it was alleged that the organisers retained control and enjoyed better food and quarters than the unemployed.[55]

These social events, taken as a whole, show that the movement was not, as some contended, an organisation in which Communists inflicted hardship on the workless by putting them through punishing Hunger Marches in the dead of winter, simply for their own political ends. Here was a different image of the NUWM, one which the leadership propagated through the film *A Holiday From Unemployment* which it had made of the Clifton Hampden site, which was shown at many meetings with the help of Kino films. It was unfortunate if understandable, then, if after 1936 and the outbreak of the Spanish Civil War, headquarters and District Councils lost their momentum in developing the NUWM's social life.[56]

The Fight Against Part Two

Unemployed activists attending summer camps in 1934 were well aware that the new Unemployment Insurance Bill contained a second part which was to be unveiled that winter. The regulations made under Part Two were not published until just before Christmas, but had already been accurately predicted by Hannington in a series of articles. Part Two and the regulations constituted a massive attack on the unemployed and the NUWM, by establishing a new body, the Unemployment Assistance Board (UAB), with six members, all appointed by the government, and funded by the state. On 7 January, all of those receiving transitional benefit were to come under the UAB; on 1 March, all of those on Poor Law relief were also to be transferred. In effect, the administration of all non-insurance benefit was to be given to a new body working within detailed legal guidelines and relatively immune to the pressures which could be put on the PACs. Scales of relief were reduced in relation to insurance scales. But, most unpalatable of all, was a new uniform Means Test regulated by extremely complicated formulae. This last measure was especially threatening, as it both institutionalised and obfuscated the workings of the hated Means Test.

When the Ninth National Conference of the NUWM met in Derby in mid-December 1934, the movement was already in action trying to improve scales of relief, and preparing itself for a massive struggle over Part Two. The Conference report was confident that the one hundred and fifty delegates were 'clear-sighted about the problems which face the movement and knew how to tackle them'.[57] Passing all the resolutions with only minor amendments, the Conference took two main decisions: to organise 'mass actions' against the new legislation, and to approach the TUC to support the NUWM in the localities and to encourage mass refusals to enter the slave camps.[58] The approach to the TUC was an important sign of the times, indicating as it did how the gradual drift away from the sectarian policies of the beginning of the decade was continuing within the Communist Party and the NUWM. Although the policies were not yet fully developed, nor were they blessed by the Comintern, there were moves towards building wider alliances within and without the labour movement. The response of the TUC, through Citrine, was that communications from the NUWM could not be answered. But the attitude of trade unionists at local level was far less bureaucratic. Indeed, the extent of the upsurge which resulted in South Wales in the New Year was clearly unexpected even by NUWM headquarters.

During 1934, the NUWM had forged new links with the SWMF as its branches played a key role in helping the miners' union in its campaign to crush the company union which remained in existence in the area. In this determined struggle to eliminate the company union, there were no 'Third Period' qualms about co-operating with the SWMF, because the enemy was clear. In the protracted dispute at the Taff-Merthyr colliery, the NUWM leafleted, picketed and recruited to a new unemployed miners' lodge, earning it the vilification of the company. NUWM branches outside of Bedlinog (Taff Merthyr's colliery village) sat on committees of the SWMF established to stop blacklegging of employed or unemployed by nipping it in the bud. It was little wonder, then, that NUWM Circulars were already praising the 'very excellent' situation at Bedlinog, where the NUWM and SWMF were virtually synonymous.[59] This unity was to bear fruit in the massive demonstrations which swept South Wales for the month after Part Two came into operation on 7 January 1935. South Wales was at the centre of a national ferment. The sense of accumulated rage which had been just below the surface since the cuts of 1931 now came bursting volcanically through. But years of experience in organising the unemployed accumulated by the NUWM since the early 1920s also showed in the demonstrations that followed. The NAC received details of the extent of the demonstrations: on 13 January, 100,000 people marched in the Rhondda, and between then and the end of the month, 150,000 participated in NUWM-led marches throughout Britain. But South Wales was the storm centre. On 3 February 300,000 people demonstrated throughout South Wales.[60] The scale of the upsurge was truly enormous. There were notable absences from the list of demonstrations, where NUWM organisation was exposed as weak; the NAC picked out London and Lancashire in particular.[61] But these mobilisations moved many people to feel that the government could not hold out under such pressure. Celebrated at the time by Ben Francis in *Unemployed Leader*, the demonstrations were also captured for eternity by Lewis Jones in his powerful novel *We Live*.

   Jones's chapter 'Cwmardy Marches' ends as the great revolt climaxed in reality: with a body of irate women storming the offices of the UAB. On Monday 4 February, the NUWM led 1,000 men and twice as many women to the UAB offices in Merthyr and rushed them, totally destroying the records within. A few clerks had been seen making faces at them from inside the building, and the crowd's response had been swift and to the point. Refusing to listen to appeals for calm, they wrecked the building, destroying records and the building's interior. The following day, Oliver Stanley, Minister of Labour, announced that the UAB scales of relief were to be suspended, and that claimants would be entitled either to UAB or PAC scales, whichever was the highest.

The NUWM was jubilant. In a circular sent out on 6 February, Hannington wrote: 'Smashing victory for the NUWM! Follow Up for complete abolition of the Act!' Announcing that 'We have scored one of the greatest victories in the history of the British working class movement,' Hannington contended that here was an 'emphatic answer' to the 'tame reformist leaders' who had said that the workers would have to wait until the next election:

> It is the most outstanding proof that has yet been given of the correctness of the line of the NUWM – its line of mass struggle based upon the unity of the unemployed workers and the bringing in of the employed workers in support of this struggle.[62]

Hannington referred to the importance of the support given by the SWMF to the NUWM in the campaign, many lodge banners having been seen at the head of demonstrations alongside those of the unemployed movement. Elias also recognised the importance of this, but could not resist pointing out that the Labour Party in Parliament had been unable to alter 'a single full stop or comma' in the regulations.[63]

Hannington insisted on the importance of carrying on the agitation in order to secure withdrawal of the entire Act. A massive demonstration in Sheffield on 6 February which ended in terrible police violence, went ahead, but this had been planned for since November.[64] In March, the movement held a march into Glasgow, which brought 3,500 unemployed from Aberdeen. But the Scottish march effectively marked the end of the wave of revolt of 1935, which had begun to decline from 5 February onwards. In retrospect, this point can be seen as a high-water mark for the unemployed movement. The NUWM had never won a clearer victory for the unemployed, and Hannington felt that the government could have been toppled at this time if the Labour Party and TUC had been determined to push for this. This assessment may be exaggerated, yet there is no doubt that retrospective attempts by the Labour Party and others to claim the credit for this victory are without foundation. The alliance with the SWMF had been important in South Wales, but the unemployed movement could claim the credit for Stanley's humiliating retraction.

Notes

1 NAC *Report*, 25-26 February 1933.
2 *Ten Lean Years*, p.95.
3 NAC *Report*, 26-27 August 1933,p.9.
4 NUWM *Monthly Bulletin*, February-March 1933; NAC *Report*, 27-28 May 1933, p.3.
5 Bruley, op.cit., pp.191, 221-6, 247; NAC *Report*, 25-26 February 1933.
6 Letters from Mr L. Smith to the author, 16 and 26 November 1984; *Unemployed Leader*, February 1933.
7 HQ Newsletters, 12 October 1935. WH/CP/AZc.
8 Interview of Mr George Freezer by Roger Spalding and Mike O'Sullivan (date unknown) (transcript kindly given to the author by interviewers).
9 Interview of Mr. B. Hudson by Sheila Saunders, 11 July 1984 (tape kindly given to the author by Sheila Saunders).
10 Ibid.
11 NAC *Report*, 27-28 August 1933,p.3.
12 Interview with the late Bill Wellings, 12 February 1973.
13 *Ten Lean Years*,pp.103-5.
14 *Daily Worker*, 20 January 1933, quoted by P. Scannell in 'Broadcasting and the Politics of Unemployment 1930-35', *Media, Culture and Society*, Vol.2, No.1., January 1980, p.18.
15 Scannell, op.cit., p.19.
16 Ibid., p.21.
17 *Weekly Worker*, 27 February 1932.
18 A. Clinton, *The Trade Union Rank and File*, Manchester 1977, p.160.
19 W. Hannington, *Crimes Against the Unemployed*, London 1932, p.11.
20 *Unemployed Special*, August 1932.
21 *Weekly Worker*, 23 January, 20 February 1932.
22 Clinton, op.cit., p.163.
23 TUC *Congress Report* 1937, p.116. At this point, the TUC claimed about 100 unemployed associations attached to Trades Councils (ibid.).
24 TUC *Congress Report* 1939, p.134.
25 NAC *Report*, 26-7 August 1933, p.2; *Main Resolutions of Eighth National Conference*, p.8; Kingsford, op.cit. pp.171-4.
26 H. McShane, *Three Days that Shook Edinburgh*, London 1933, p.18.

27 P. Harker, *Lancashire's Fight For Bread*, London 1933, p.1.
28 *Ten Lean Years*, p.106.
29 *Unemployed Leader*, 21 October 1933; W. Hannington, *An Exposure of the Unemployed Social Service Schemes*, London 1933.
30 Kingsford, op.cit., p.175.
31 D. Low, 'A Portrait of Wal Hannington', unpublished dissertation, Ruskin College Oxford, 1984, Chapters 3 and 4.
32 Circular C87, 13 March 1934 (WH/CP/A2d).
33 Police report, National Museum of Labour History, SBHM 100.
34 *Never On Our Knees*, pp.292-3.
35 Francis and Smith, op.cit., p.253.
36 'Notes of a Preliminary Meeting on the Hunger Marchers, 25 January 1934' National Museum of Labour History, SBHM 46 (i).
37 R. Hayburn, 'The Police and the Hunger Marchers', *International Review of Social History*, vol.xvii, 1972, Part 3, pp.625-44.
38 NAC *Report*, 23-24 January 1932.
39 Interview with Sid Elias, 7 April 1984.
40 Police report 25 February 1934 (National Museum of Labour History SBHM 145).
41 *Unemployed Leader*, May 1934.
42 *The NUWM Searchlight*, May 1935 (WH/MML/AV).
43 W. Hannington, *The Problem of the Distressed Areas*, London 1937, p.110.
44 *Unemployed Leader*, April 1935.
45 D. Colledge and J. Field, 'To Recondition Human Material. An Account of a British Labour Camp in the 1930s', *History Workshop Journal*, No.15, Spring 1983, p.162.
46 *Weekly Worker*, 5 November 1932.
47 *Unemployed Leader*, 2 December 1933.
48 Ibid., October 1934.
49 *Unemployment, Labour and Social Services Bulletin*, No.7,3 June 1938 (WH/CP/AI)
50 Christopher Brunel to Hannington 15 December 1962 (WH/CP/A4).
51 H.Marks, 'Unemployment and Adult Education in the 1930s', *Studies in Adult Education*, September 1982, p.4.
52 Pilgrim Trust, *Men Without Work,* London and New York 1938, pp.272ff.
53 NAC *Report*, 27-8 May, 26-7 August 1933.
54 *Unemployed Leader*, September 1934.
55 Ibid., September 1935.
56 'Film Shows for the Unemployed', 9 December 1935 (WH/CP/A2d).
57 Report of the Ninth National Conference, p.1. Circular D23 13 December 1934 (WH/CP/A2a).
58 Circular D/23, 13 December 1934.
59 'An Example for all South Wales Branches' (WH/CP/A2d).
60 NAC *Report* 9-10 February 1935, pp.3-5.
61 Ibid.
62 Circular D/39, 6 February 1935 (WH/CP/A2a)
63 *Unemployed Leader*, January 1935.
64 Talk by Bill Moore at History Workshop, Sheffield, 1982. Tape in author's possession.

8

From Mass Action to Token Protest, 1935-39

The NUWM in 1935

The movement's mass agitation against the government's plans to restructure the benefits system brought a massive influx of members. During the three months up to the withdrawal of Part Two, 52 new branches were formed (many of them in South Wales and Scotland); on some days, headquarters was sending out 1,000 new membership cards. This mushroom growth continued for a few weeks after the victory of 7 February; in the next month, 29 new branches sprang up. Headquarters claimed that by the spring of 1935 the membership was twice that at the time of the 1934 Conference. It seems probable, then, even if these estimates are taken as exaggerations, that the total membership was in excess of 100,000 at this point.[1]

The NAC was especially pleased to note the 'very marked' involvement of women in the wave of demonstrations.[2] This time it was accompanied by an increase in women's participation in the NUWM. Well attended women's conferences were held in Scotland, and in Nottinghamshire and Derby during the first half of the year. The Nottinghamshire and Derby Conference included delegates from a wide range of women's organisations such as the Co-op Women's Guild as well as the NUWM. Particular interest was shown in questions surrounding birth control and maternity benefits. The Conference demanded a change in the wording of the Maternity and Child Welfare Act of 1918 which would make it compulsory for local authorities to ensure the highest degree of health among expectant and nursing mothers.[3]

Local action reflected similar concerns. Just a few months after this conference, Blackpool NUWM women represented four women needing milk from a local clinic, and in Arbroath the small women's section demonstrated for a new maternity hospital.[4]

Early 1935 saw large sales of two new NUWM pamphlets which highlighted the effects of poverty on the one hand and grotesque social inequality on the other: Maud Brown's *Stop This Starvation of Mother and Child* and Hannington's *'Jubilee' Chimp – Her Birth, Food and Drink*. Maud Brown's pamphlet presented a wealth of medical evidence to show the close relationship between poverty and mother and child morbidity. The pamphlet related well to the developing movement for family allowances, and brought forward the NUWM's demands for improved relief. Hannington's penny pamphlet was a masterpiece of irony, showing the expense lavished on a chimpanzee named in honour of the royal Jubilee celebrations of 1935 in relation to the treatment of the unemployed and their children. The inequality in British society extended, as he showed, to create a gap between animals and unemployed humans. It was a contradiction which Hannington high-lighted brilliantly. The movement's propagandists were beginning to hit their targets instead of issuing, as they had tended to only a few years previously, booklets which read like extended Comintern resolutions.

Towards a British Popular Front?

The summer of 1935 brought a dramatic change in Communist politics which had in some senses been anticipated by the NUWM's alliance with the South Wales miners and their communities. The French Communists and Socialists had united to defeat the forces of the right, and Stalin recognised the validity of the French strategy in May 1935. In July 1935, the Communist International began meeting in a World Congress to ratify the new policies. In his keynote speech, Dimitrov, the Bulgarian Communist who had earned fame by successfully defending himself in a Nazi court against the charge of starting the Reichstag fire, set the tone. He announced that the old line of sectarianism towards social democracy had been jettisoned. The way forward lay in mass action in collaboration with all forces prepared to fight fascism. It also lay in attacking fascism from within, by the tactic of the 'Trojan Horse', by which fascist societies would be infiltrated and subverted. The new line was greeted by the Western Communist parties with enthusiasm and relief. Relentless struggle against the entire institutional apparatus and repressive force of the status quo, which meant imprisonment, police violence and isolation, had brought British Communists almost to the point of exhaustion and extinction by 1932. Despite their *de facto* drift away from 'Third Period' policies, they had remained an embattled grouping with strong residual elements of sectarianism. But here was an agreeable prospect: that of swimming with the stream. The new sensibility was characterised by an increased openness. Communists adopted a more conciliatory vocabulary towards their neighbours on the left, and began a tireless search for liaisons with anyone who would join with them on however minimal a basis of agreement. The fight against fascism became everything, and as the decade continued the spirit of a Popular Front became increasingly pervasive on the British left.

The new line, because it encouraged the Communist Party to adopt more broadly based policies within the NUWM, could be seen as encouraging. But there was a more important sense in which it threatened the very existence of the organisation. There were some influential Communist militants in the NUWM who, even before the new line was ratified by the Communist International, had drawn the conclusion that there was no longer any need for 'divisive' movements like the NUWM. The principal arguments in this direction came from South Wales, where there had always been a strong current of opinion favouring organisation of the unemployed through the miners' lodges. The experience of the winter of 1934-35 had seemed to strengthen this thesis as a movement of unemployed and employed had been co-ordinated by and channelled through the Miners' Federation. At a meeting of the Welsh Council of the NUWM held in late June 1935, Lewis Jones had, according at least to a headquarters circular, 'made statements that amounted to an advocacy for the liquidation of the NUWM branches in South Wales, favouring either Labour Party Unemployed Associations or Unemployed Sections of

Miners' Lodges'.[5] Headquarters was quick to repudiate this 'line of liquidation' and to instruct members on the need to build the NUWM. Jones continued to participate in the NUWM, but the impression of uncertainty over whether the movement should continue to exist in the new political circumstances was debilitating to the membership as a whole.

The national line found support in South Wales from NUWM members whose local SWMF lodges remained hostile and refused to allow them to join. Unemployed lodges were not always sympathetic to the NUWM, as George Brown, an old activist from the area explained, 'There wasn't a snowball's chance in hell' of getting into the lodge unless they had a job in the pit. The unemployed lodge was made up of people who were 'the worst element of the unemployed, I would say they weren't prepared to struggle for that then', but were simply waiting for the day when union membership would help them find work again. Such people were not prepared to lessen their chances of work by allowing known agitators into their ranks. In the circumstances, the majority of South Walian NUWM members rejected the view of their popular leader.[6]

Nor was Jones's line a momentary and individual aberration. In early 1936, the Communist leader Harry Pollitt, was advocating 'One united unemployed association'.[7] It was hardly surprising if, by 1938, party leaders were criticising a 'false interpretation' of Communist Party policy which was leading some members to build unemployed associations rather than the NUWM.[8] Pollitt's phrase was studied in its ambivalence, and indicated an apparent lack of enthusiasm for a separate Communist-led unemployed movement which was transmitted to the party rank and file. The high level of undivided commitment and self-sacrifice which had for so long sustained the movement was, from 1935, being shared with other organisations. The Northampton branch of the NUWM, writing to the Trades Council in an attempt to merge with its unemployed association, pointed out with some justification and a certain sense of grievance, that it thought its approach

> The very apex of renunciation ... Considering the NUWM has done all the spade work in the past and being the only real National Movement for the unemployed, we are ready to

sacrifice our individual movement and amalgamate into one
big party ...⁹

The new Communist Party policy for all its potential
advantages, could mean, in some areas at least, that the
NUWM was not so much forming tactical alliances with
unemployed associations, as effectively dissolving itself. This,
it was clearly felt by some, was the only way to obtain the
maximum unity which the situation demanded. It was a
disastrous interpretation for the NUWM as an organisation.

From the 1935 General Election to the 1936 Hunger March

The new line had taken root firmly by the autumn preceding
the 1935 General Election. Within the NUWM, the attitude to
the Labour Party in local and parliamentary elections had
changed dramatically. Whereas during the whole of the
period from the Seventh National Conference to late 1934 the
NUWM had taken the attitude that where no candidate could
satisfy the movement's requirements the NUWM should back
a 'Workers' Candidate' (not an NUWM candidate, which was
considered too narrow), it now supported the Labour Party
where there was no Communist candidate. During the 1935
General Election, the NUWM helped the Labour candidates
in practically every constituency, and headquarters com-
mented on the 'very excellent picture' of collaboration which
they had, and on the many letters of thanks which they had
received from Labour Party organisations all over the
country.¹⁰ The Labour Party recovered somewhat from its
very poor position in this election; Labour candidates were
returned in 154 seats, three times the number won in 1931.
The government remained essentially Conservative despite
the 'National' label retained for electoral convenience.

Not surprisingly, relations with the Labour Party improved
in the new climate. This was particularly important to
NUWM members where the Labour Party had members on
Courts of Referees and Appeals Tribunals. The NUWM was
increasingly able to co-operate with some of these people and
to ask them to exchange information in the interests of the
claimant. Nationally, the unemployed movement organised
meetings of these representatives. It asked them to regard

themselves as delegates of the labour movement rather than as
impartial judges, to refuse to disallow anyone on any grounds
and to demand the records of allowances and disallowances
made by particular bodies so that campaigns could be
initiated to remove 'vicious chairmen'.[11] Close links were
developed in several areas, with excellent results for the
unemployed.

A similar shift in attitude towards the TUC was also in
evidence in this period. At the beginning of 1935, the NAC
had circulated correspondence with Citrine to trade union
bodies to show the way that the TUC was 'deliberately
splitting the workers' front'.[12] By September, the NAC was
applauding the TUC's criticism of the NCSS centres, and
arguing that TUC-sponsored unemployed associations should
be treated fraternally.[13] But bridges were not that easily
repaired, and the NUWM was still treated with suspicion and
some cynicism by trade union leaders. At the TUC
Conference of 1935, for example, Donovan of the TGWU
accused the NUWM of offering to supply scab labour during
several recent industrial disputes. The movement's headquarters immediately denied the accusation. In reply, it
circulated a document listing the movement's activities in
disputes. It pointed to the Taff Merthyr battle in South
Wales; to a strike by the National Federation of Retail
Newsagents after which the movement was publicly thanked
in the Federation's National *News-sheet* for its help; to support
for the West Wales bus strike in May 1935; to action taken in
Kent to help the ETU demand the reinstatement of a sacked
shop steward.[14] If anything, headquarters had understated its
case, but this was hardly the point. The accusation had been
made, and was an indication of the continued bad feeling
against the NUWM by some trade union leaders. This
naturally made life more difficult at local level. Although there
was an increasing tendency for the TUC's unemployed
associations to link up with the NUWM, there were some
trade unionists who could not forget the earlier attacks made
on their 'reformist' leaders and on their own organisations.
There were some who agreed with Ernie Bevin, that the trade
unions had no reason to support what he described to Citrine
as Hannington's 'move ... to get into the Movement again'.[15]
The NUWM ploughed on, trying to stress areas in which

co-operation was possible, but without official recognition there were, as Hannington realised, strict limitations to what could be achieved locally.

The new line nevertheless brought real gains in terms of the support offered to the 1936 Hunger Marchers. The London Trades Council was a sponsor of the march, as were many Labour Party and trade union bodies. Symbolically, Aneurin Bevan, last involved with the NUWM as a delegate to the Stoke-on-Trent Conference in 1925, was now a member of the reception committee. The police reports stressed that the Communist Party had decided that the 'party character' of the march was to be kept in the background, and that it was to be made an 'all-in' protest. The police, mindful of the widespread support for the march, decided to treat the marchers tactfully: if marchers were suspected of having offensive weapons, then the contingent leader was to be approached rather than the individual concerned.[16] The police were right to treat the march with circumspection: not only was it the biggest of all the marches between the wars, with nearly 1,500 participating, it also contained a large number of public figures. There were two dozen councillors in the Welsh contingent alone.[17]

The marchers of the NUWM had decided that the attacks on the unemployed contained in new regulations published in July called for a militant response. The Means Test had been made a permanent feature, and cuts in benefit had been imposed in relation to transitional payments. But the Jarrow Town Council decided to organise a march to London which would specifically define itself against the NUWM's spirit of political militancy. Whilst the NUWM leadership was prepared to associate itself with broad political demands, such as support for the Republican government in Spain, the Jarrow Council rejected such associations, preferring to emphasise the town's plight in a narrow and localised way, and without making any other political demands. The NUWM, meanwhile, made every effort to avoid any hint of criticism of the Jarrow march. Wal Hannington, who of course had enormous experience of organising marches, was consulted by Ellen Wilkinson, Labour MP for Jarrow, and had taken the opportunity to suggest that the Jarrow Crusade should be co-ordinated and associated with that of the NUWM.

Wilkinson had passed on the suggestion to the Jarrow
Council, but had seen it rejected.[18] The Jarrow Council knew
very well the nature of the NUWM; the town had for many
years had a very active NUWM branch which had organised
protests against the activities of some of the councillors. The
Jarrow Crusade attracted press interest and support from
many who were pleased to see an alternative to the NUWM.
Philanthropic gestures were forthcoming from such as Sir
John Jarvis, who paid for the men to have a steamer trip on
the Thames (a trip which might have been considered a
studied insult to ex-shipyard workers) and Sir Albert Levy,
who paid £100 for the replacement of the men's clothes. But
the humble petitioners hardly managed to obtain a hearing for
Sir Nicholas Grattan-Doyle who presented their petition to
the House of Commons. The government certainly made no
concessions.

Despite their initial rejection, the Communist Party and the
NUWM made every effort to support the Jarrow Crusade.
Ellen Wilkinson, in her famous book on Jarrow, *The Town
That Was Murdered*, praised the party's generosity in offering
the Crusaders the support of its meeting held in Hyde Park to
receive the Hunger Marchers. Much less well known is the
active support for the Crusaders provided by a small group of
NUWM members. John Jackson, the keen NUWMer from
Birkenhead had tried, with a group of unemployed comrades
about twenty strong, to travel to France to join those already
fighting in defence of the Spanish Republic, but had been
foiled by a close police tail. Returning to Manchester, the
group discussed what they could do together. John recalled:

> So we decided that what we would do, that eighteen or so of us,
> we set off from Manchester, and we went under our own steam
> towards London because in those days certain chaps who were
> on the real dole could get what they called a travelling card
> and we pooled what resources we had ... and then what we
> did, we got ahead, or behind, of the Jarrow marchers and tried
> to organise meetings outside the Labour Exchanges in the
> various places which the Jarrow marchers would come
> through, to try and stir up a doings. Then when we got near to
> London, we were ahead of the Jarrow marchers, so what we
> did, we lay back, and we let the Jarrow march go in and we
> went into London under our own steam, but the NUWM in

London knew we were there. That was the day. Coming from the provinces like I had, and I'd never been in a place like London in my life, I never saw so many policemen in my life, I, honestly, *never*, I didn't imagine there was that many in the world. But then when we got in we split up and went to various areas of the NUWM in London. I was attached to Southwark most of the time and we joined in there.[19]

Here, then, was the spirit of the Popular Front manifested within the rank and file of the movement: even while their own march was on, John Jackson and his comrades were supporting the non-political Crusaders at no small cost to themselves. The politics of self-effacement were being lived out by even the most militant members of the NUWM. Lewis Jones must have approved, having pushed the logic one step further.

The NUWM Hunger Marchers also adopted a policy of a 'broad front' which brought considerable support from the Labour Party. Whilst the *Daily Herald* reported a Hunger March favourably for the first time since 1922, Clement Attlee argued for the marchers to be allowed to present their petition at the bar of the House of Commons. Conscious of the support behind them, the march leaders now showed the crucial difference between themselves and the Jarrow Crusaders. The NUWM insisted that it would see a Cabinet Minister, and a deputation of march leaders was scheduled to visit 10 Downing Street when it heard from Willie Gallacher, the Scottish Communist MP elected in 1935, and Aneurin Bevan, that the Minister of Labour would meet those two MPs with a deputation of Hunger Marchers.[20] At this meeting, the Minister made an important concession. The scales of relief which were due to be implemented four days later would be postponed for two months. In addition, those who were due to have increases to benefit under the new regulations would have them immediately, whilst those who were to have reductions would have them phased in over a period of eighteen months. Such concessions could hardly be portrayed as matters of detail; they were clearly the result of militant action by the NUWM and to that extent were proof of the *Manchester Guardian*'s argument that the Jarrow Crusaders had not made themselves 'nuisance enough'.[21]

Although the NUWM's militant approach had been amply
justified by events, it was the Jarrow Crusade that lived on
as the symbol of unemployed action in the 1930s, as the
officially approved motif of 'peaceful protest'. This is an
historical injustice of the first order which has been reproduced
by labour-movement historians who might have been
expected to approach the matter more critically.[22] It is
important to note that the political space for a 'moderate'
march like that from Jarrow had been created by the
campaigns of the NUWM. The Conservative Party provided
hospitality for the men at Sheffield, Nottingham and
Chesterfield. Just as it was no accident that the marchers
came from Jarrow, nor was it surprising that the Tories
should support the Jarrow men in these three towns, because
in each of them the NUWM had for years sustained a
tradition of uncompromising struggle based firmly on the
demands of the national movement.

The Roots of Decline

Hunger Marches were often followed by periods of
quiescence,and this was particularly noticeable after the 1936
march. On this occasion, however, it was not simply a short
period of exhaustion that was apparent, but rather the
beginning of a longer-term decline. From being a mass
movement involving tens of thousands, the NUWM became a
small residual body carrying out propaganda and publicity
'stunts' on behalf of the unemployed.

The organisation had been in serious financial difficulties
even before the Hunger March. By November 1935,
Hannington had to inform branches that the services of three
national propagandists (Emryhs Llewellyn, Don Melville and
Ted Williams) had all been recently lost due to lack of money.
In addition, two members of the office staff had been laid off
for the same reason. This left only Hannington, McShane and
Elias available for national organising.[23] Income was a chronic
problem in the movement because of the difficulty of retaining
people as regular dues-paying members after a wave of mass
involvement. The uncertainty of life as an unemployed
worker, and extreme poverty, made it difficult for the workless
to maintain their financial commitment to the NUWM. This

had always been a problem. The new element, which led to indebtedness, had been the practice of deficit financing, particularly of the legal work and the intermittent *Unemployed Leader*. Whilst branches showed a declining interest in paying both the legal levy and for sufficient copies of the paper, the national office kept on engaging lawyers and publishing the paper. There was a limit to the credit which could be extended to branches and now it had been reached. The problem of limited local loyalty to the national office, so often pointed out by the headquarters officials, had come home to roost.

This problem had been recognised for many years, but its solution had only served to exacerbate the difficulty. Making the paper a national organ, allowing the leadership to dominate the national conference and issuing a stream of headquarters directives to branches, did not have the desired effect since none of these strategies really sought to involve the membership in a genuine discussion about the best way forward for the organisation. Thus, although it was true that in some senses the centralisation strategy succeeded in building an effective organisation (Hunger Marches became steadily better organised, for example), it was a failure in the financial sense.

An additional 'problem' for the movement was the fall in the number of potential recruits, since unemployment declined from 1934 onwards. At its lowest, it stood at 1,334,000 in the autumn of 1937. Unemployment was being reduced particularly quickly in the manufacturing areas where rearmament was proceeding apace. The extractive industries, however, remained in difficulties. The result was a differential pattern of activism for the movement which was deprived of some of its best cadres in engineering centres whilst remaining relatively strong in mining regions. The upturn in the arms industries eroded one of the main networks on which the NUWM had been built and maintained: the AEU skilled engineers, and the effects of this can hardly be exaggerated. In Lancashire, the majority of NUWM activists gained employment in the mid-1930s.[24] The AEU and the shop stewards' movement had gained at the expense of the NUWM.

Just after the end of the 1936 Hunger March, the movement lost its chairman in disconcerting circumstances, further depleting the human resources available to the NUWM

nationally. During the Hunger March, the anti-Communist
Economic League had put out a leaflet which claimed that Sid
Elias had offered to provide it with information on the
movement's activities. Harry Pollitt drew this to Hannington's
attention, and they asked the Economic League for a copy of
Elias's letter. A photocopy was supplied, and Hannington
reported to the NAC that its chairman could no longer be
trusted. Elias denies the accusation to this day, and the case
against him is indeed not proven. The records of the Economic
League are not extant for this period, but the obvious question
remains: if Elias had offered his services to the League, then
why did it not accept? Given the emphasis the League placed
on anti-Communist propaganda, surely such a contact would
have been very valuable? In any case, the effect of the
accusation was damaging and demoralising, particularly since
it raised the further obvious question: was Elias the police spy
on the NAC? It was a shattering question for those involved in
the movement to have to ask themselves. The only individual
of greater standing in the movement was Hannington himself.
Elias had been involved with the movement since its earliest
days with the exception of a period of employment in the
mid-1920s, and had provided legal advice for almost every
branch. Now the possibility arose that he might have been a
Judas.[25]

'Unemployed Struggles'

By the end of 1936, Hannington's book *Unemployed Struggles*
had been published, marking its author's recognition that the
era of mass unemployed struggles had come to an end. At the
NAC meeting held at the beginning of July 1936, it was
recorded in the report to branches that Hannington had

> recently finished writing a book that gives a complete history of
> the struggles of the unemployed and the work of our movement
> since the end of the war ... This book fills a very important gap
> in British Working Class History; it makes an exciting story
> from beginning to end; it is not written in a dry, academic way,
> but is enlivened by many exciting experiences which are
> recorded therein.[26]

These comments, which accurately reflect the book as we

know it, were made of a manuscript of 150,000 words, which was much longer than the published text.[27] *Unemployed Struggles* was sold internally to the NUWM in a special cheap edition costing 2s.6d, and was also available to trade union branches at that price. The NAC suggested that the text should be made the basis for discussion in the branches, and that the more expensive 10s.6d edition should be made the prize in raffles and draws runs locally. Lawrence and Wishart were able to report a good sale and praise from many in the literary world.[28]

In a decade of literary achievement by working-class writers, Hannington made a mark for himself with *Unemployed Struggles*. Although he lacked the vivid expressive abilities of Lewis Jones or Walter Brierley, he showed himself well able to develop a racy and inspiring narrative based on his own experiences. Meticulous as ever, he began by consulting his volumes of newspaper cuttings which he had maintained over the years. From these articles he was able to reconstruct the movement's activities without falling into the trap of exaggerating his own role in events, unlike many of his Communist contemporaries. The book has become a labour movement classic, well received by those who participated in the struggles, and a beacon for those who have had no experience of agitation among the workless.

The favourable reaction to the publication of *Unemployed Struggles* showed that Hannington had made the transition from being an able journalist and pamphleteer to being a successful author. Encouraged, he went on to develop his new found skill. He began work on a book with a polemical and campaigning purpose, which was published in 1937 as *The Problem of the Distressed Areas*. This was a systematic critique of official policy towards the so-called 'Distressed Areas' which was widely discussed beyond Communist circles, and an important contribution to the debate on public health and welfare in the decade of unemployment.

Now that the movement was no longer in a position to contest every issue through agitation on a large scale, Hannington was adapting and continuing the struggle by other means. He was now making an impact within informed discussion, with all the authority of years of experience among the unemployed behind him. It was a remarkably successful change in the focus of his activity, and one which he achieved without ever abandoning the option of action on the streets and outside the Labour Exchanges.

Hannington's personal circumstances had changed since the early 1930s. Now approaching forty, he had been imprisoned for the last time. He and Winnie had moved from their flat in Hampstead and were living in a new house in Colindale. Travel was also becoming easier: he had the occasional use of a car lent him by a sympathetic comrade, and later acquired his own dilapidated Morris.[29] Hannington remained very much the working-class Communist militant, but his position had changed greatly from the early days of the unemployed movement; he would not be approaching the pawn shop with his boxing cups again. His position as National Organiser of the NUWM was secure, his life-style not dissimilar to that of a trade union official. Increasingly, the lead was being taken by others in the NUWM as Hannington slowed down somewhat.

The NUWM, the Spanish Civil War and the Fight Against Fascism

In the period after the end of the 1936 Hunger March, unemployed agitation assumed less importance in the Communist Party's priorities. By October 1936, the International Brigades were being formed for the defence of the Republic and Harry Pollitt was recruiting to the British contingent through his *Daily Worker* column. The NAC became fully committed to the defence of the Spanish Republic when, in August 1936, it expressed its collective disturbance at the 'false neutrality' of the British government.[30] This was an important departure for the NAC, which had previously held that the NUWM should be wary of taking positions which might alienate non-Communists. At the time of the Abyssinian crisis, for example, the NAC had reacted cautiously, circulating branches to ask whether its position of opposition to the Italian invasion met with their approval.[31] The NAC's decision to take a public stance was justified at the Tenth National Conference, receiving the 'almost unanimous support' of the delegates.[32] In the case of Spain, there were no such agonisings; it was felt to be essential to take a stand for the Spanish Republic and against the rising tide of fascism.

The unemployed movement had good reason for taking a determined stand against fascism, deriving directly from experience that stretched back into the 1920s. As a movement which was very public in the sense that it made itself visible on the streets at every opportunity, it had been subjected to periodic attacks by small groups of *'fascisti'*, who saw an opportunity of attacking 'Communists'. In 1929, the NUWM's headquarters had been ransacked and daubed with fascist slogans. During the 1930s, Mosley's British Union of Fascist (BUF) posed a more serious threat to the NUWM. As a larger and more coherent organisation than the tiny and faintly ridiculous groups of British *'fascisti'*, it was able to mount both a political challenge to the unemployed movement as a rival for the allegiance of the workless, and a serious physical threat. Thorough examination of the newspapers of the extreme right brought no substantial evidence of defections from the NUWM to the BUF. In this, the situation was different to that in Germany in the early 1930s, when some sizeable groups of unemployed moved over from the German Communists to the Nazi Party. Nevertheless, the main threat lay not so much in this direction as in the possibility that the BUF could recruit effectively amongst those unemployed who were untouched by the NUWM, and turn them against the Communist-led movement. In this sense, the BUF always had to be taken seriously by the NUWM, even after the famous 'Battle of Cable Street' in which the BUF had its progress stopped both physically and symbolically in the East End of London. The NUWM played no small part in the Cable Street success, but could never afford to write the BUF off completely, and therefore took increasing pains to make its anti-fascist stance crystal clear to the unemployed, with unemployed demands often being put next to anti-fascist slogans.

A major reason for the NUWM's commitment to the cause of the Spanish Republic, as distinct from anti-fascism more generally, was the emphasis put on the issue by the international Communist movement. Whilst there had been occasions in the early 1930s on which the unemployed movement's leadership had maintained a discreet distance from some of the Communist Party's policies, this was not the case with Spain. Nothing was to be spared in the fight for democracy in Spain, and the NUWM paid the price for this stand. The contribution made by the movement to the International Brigades was large indeed. In South Wales alone, 37 of the volunteers were veterans of Hunger Marches.[33] Of the 2,000 British volunteers, it is impossible to say exactly how many were members of the NUWM, but the answer would probably run into several hundreds. The unemployed often felt they had nothing to lose by going. Their movement, on the other hand, had much to lose, with many of their activists being taken out of the unemployed arena for the duration. The casualty rate amongst volunteers was very high, and by October 1937 three members of the NAC (Bob Elliott, Wilf Jobling and Eric Whalley) had been killed.[34] The NAC invariably opened its meetings by observing a minute's silence for comrades killed in action.

Enthusiasm for the fight against fascism led the movement in directions that were questionable in terms of its own principles. The Hawick branch's scheme for providing woollen goods for Spain, adopted by the NUWM nationally, was a case in point. When the sympathetic owner of a woollen mill rented the Hawick branch part of his disused building to serve as branch premises, the ex-woollen workers in the branch saw the potential of the idle machinery. Then the need of the Spanish Republic for woollen goods caught their eye, and Councillor Stoddart of the branch travelled to London to discuss the idea with Hannington. On 31 December 1936, an appeal was made in the *Daily Worker* for funds to help the branch begin to operate the mill as a co-operative business to provide woollen goods for the Spanish Republic. In January 1937, Hannington made a further appeal for money to support the scheme. At the Tenth National Conference held in April 1937, a resolution called on all branches to raise a minimum of 5s. per week to help the Hawick enterprise.[35] The mill was run on a non-profit making basis, with a committee running the business, a canteen, and so on.[36] Some of those who worked were paid, but others worked for nothing.[37] This last aspect raised at least two issues for the unemployed movement. If NUWM members were going to accept work for no wages, did not this undermine their traditional insistence that the unemployed should only accept work at trade union rates of pay? Being accused of failing to practice what it preached was always dangerous for the NUWM, which had little but consistency and moral authority in its favour. In any case, was the establishment of co-operatives the general direction which the movement should have been taking? Did this development tend to detract from the unremitting agitation which had always received such emphasis in the NUWM? Such questions may have been asked at the Tenth National Conference, but the report of that conference, in common with the other conference reports of the 1930s, did not summarise debates.

The Unemployment Research and Advice Bureau

Lack of money made it impossible to employ a national office worker to replace Sid Elias in order to carry on the legal side of the movement's activities. During 1937, it had been decided to establish a separate organisation to carry on this work, and in early 1938 the Unemployment Research and Advice Bureau (URAB) was formed and began producing a *Bulletin*. URAB was staffed by legal experts, many of whom, like John Lewis, had a history of association with the unemployed movement. Its *Bulletin* appeared at monthly intervals and contained a couple of pages of legal information about unemployed allowances, legal decisions, and so on. The *Bulletin* was circulated to subscribing bodies such as union branches, public libraries, campaigning groups and NUWM branches. At times, the *Bulletin* came quite close to being an informal NUWM paper, in that it regularly reported activities which it approved of; in April 1939, for example, it reported the way that NUWM members had been organised to provide support and representation to groups of strikers from the Siemens works in London.[38] It could not, however, be a complete substitute for the movement's own paper and never claimed any such status.

The URAB was in a sense a substitute for the NUWM's own legal department, but it was also typical of these years in that it took points concerning welfare to a rather different audience to that addressed by the NUWM. By becoming a part of the 1930s 'welfare lobby' of professionals in medicine, law and public policy, it sought to shift attitudes within that influential sector in the manner of a 'pressure group'. In this sense, it could be seen as a useful adjunct to the NUWM, and as a precursor of many later organisations.

Spectacular Action By the Few

In the last two years before the outbreak of the Second World War, the movement suffered from a slow but steady drain of activists into work and other political activity. The membership base was being eroded and there were probably no more than 100 functioning branches at this time, many of which were run by just a few members. Such a situation brought its own problems, not the least of which was the difficulties involved in maintaining some sort of democracy at branch level. One branch officer wrote in June 1939 that a rather secretive NUWM claims officer had to be treated carefully so as not to hurt his feelings. Unsuccessful cases should not be mentioned, 'as he is at the moment the whole of the claims committee. Most of our committee that was, is at work, and the branch is being run, as it were, autocratically, by about four of us.'[39] Soon afterwards, Henry Birkett of the Romford branch wrote to headquarters saying that he was going to take action by himself, 'not to be undemocratic, but because I realise that action in this case is vital urgent'. There was a need to arouse some activity amongst the members, 'these lethargic people'.[40]

The trend towards an organisation in which the headquarters determined everything was accelerated by this decline in branch activity. This had been reflected at the 1937 conference in Blackpool, its tenth and last. A great deal of time was apparently spent on a long 'main resolution' proposed by Hannington, followed by a resolution put forward by the NAC calling on branches to respond to their suggested National Petition on unemployment. Maud Brown proposed a resolution on women, Harry McShane one on Spain, and so on. There were just seven resolutions from branches. None of them dealt with the main strategic issues confronting the movement.[41] The involvement of delegates occurred strictly within the parameters laid down by headquarters. The contrast with the conferences of the 1920s could hardly have been greater. Where the earlier gatherings had been lively, vigorous and even unruly, the later conferences were comparatively formal, stage-managed and platform-led.

The activity of the movement in these last years was also very much led from the centre. A campaign of 'stunts' was organised to give publicity to the NUWM's demand for increased winter relief. Don Renton, the movement's new London Organiser, was the prime motive force behind the London stunts. Renton had first become involved in the NUWM in Edinburgh in 1926 when he was just fourteen. He fought with the British Battalion in Spain, becoming a Political Commissar despite his youth. Taken prisoner by the Nationalists, he was imprisoned, but then had the good fortune to be exchanged for a Francoist prisoner. The stunts campaign bore the mark of Renton's military experience. The tactic required imagination, daring, initiative, and, above all, secrecy, so that the authorities could not head off the planned operation. Those taking part very often did not know until the last minute what they were to do, and their state of tense excitement can be imagined. People were asked to simply follow the organisers' orders. On 21 December 1938, for example, a group of men were told to collect posters, assemble in groups and gather together at a certain point in Oxford Street. Then they were suddenly told to lie down in the middle of a major junction, covered by their posters, in the fifteen seconds' grace given by the traffic lights. It was an operation requiring some courage and discipline, but the reaction was immediate and effective.[42] At this time, the campaign was quite intensive. On 22 December, there was an 'invasion' of the Ritz in which 50 unemployed went in, sat down, and asked for tea explaining that they could not pay; soon afterwards, fifteen men presented a petition to the king; on New Year's Eve, banners inscribed 'For a Happy New Year the Unemployed Must Not Starve in 1939' were suspended from the top of the Monument, and a coffin was paraded around Piccadilly Circus marked 'He did not get winter relief'.[43] In other actions men chained themselves to the railings outside the UAB offices. As winter gave way to spring, the protests took on a more anti-fascist character, and in late March 1939, a demonstration took place outside the fascist 'Brown House' in Paddington. The slogans carried by the demonstrators included 'Work for British Unemployed – Not Slave Camps. Clear out the Nazis'.[44]

The stunts campaign was not restricted to London, although the capital was its centre. In his account of the Nottingham branch's work presented in fictional form, Harry Davies recounted one such incident in which the Area UAB offices were raided. First of all, the Area Officer had to be found, as the location of his office was kept secret. Whilst a member with an Oxford accent (a sprinkling of such people joined the movement in the late 1930s) used his cultural advantage to locate the office, three men and three women were chosen for the raid. It was decided to leave the job to the three women. As a distraction, a well advertised public meeting was held in the Old Market Square with two speakers known to the police. The three women meanwhile took the Area Officer by surprise. After a quiet knock ('He was a very important man. Not to be disturbed under any circumstances.'), the women crashed in, seized his key and disconnected the phone. Hanging their banner reading 'We Refuse to Starve in Silence' out of the window, they proceeded to present their case for improved winter relief to the Area Officer. When the police arrived, the women were roughly evicted, but according to Davies there was some improvement in the officer's decisions from that point onwards: 'The raid had penetrated the cold heart of the UAB.'[45]

Unemployed Communists were still active in some localities, setting up and running new branches, despite the small numbers prepared to follow their lead. In Inverness, for example, Tom McKay, then a young Communist railway clerk, joined the NUWM branch formed in the summer of 1938 by the Jewish tailor Mark Cymbalist and the pugnacious Jim Cochrane. The new branch soon grew to 50 paying members and carried on lively business meetings, imaginative representational work (whole families were taken to the PAC and stayed until their cases were dealt with satisfactorily), and ran big children's Christmas parties. The branch even played its part in leading off an NUWM march from Inverness to Edinburgh in the winter of 1938-39. Tom McKay, prevented from marching beyond Nairn by his irate father, recounted the way in which the contingent was made to look bigger than it actually was:

We had a truck, that went up to Nairn ... So, how many actually marched? Possibly not more than a dozen. They were picking up people all the way and of course in Aberdeen they would have picked up a fair contingent ... but of course there was a lot of bloody people went to Nairn, because there was a truck there to take them back, you see [laughing]. You know how these things start off, you start off marching and there's a hell of a lot but of course they never go very far. By the time we reached Dalcross, which is four miles, five miles out of Inverness, they were going back ... It's the old story, you summon, you get as many people as possible and you set off and march up the road – this of course gets the headlines in the press 'Marchers Off To Aberdeen' and a photograph appears in the paper and, you know, you think there's 500 people marching [laughing]. In fact, you've got a dozen![46]

The Inverness branch may have used such ruses, but it was nevertheless a persistent little group that remained active until the very end of the NUWM a few years later.

Like those involved in the 'stunts', the activists involved in Inverness had found a way of protesting effectively with small numbers. The NUWM was continuing its tradition of providing an outlet for those unemployed who were willing to fight despite the difficulties. Pressure was kept on the government at a time when they might have been tempted to inflict further cuts on the unemployed whilst the public's attention was distracted by the tense international situation. By the late summer of 1939, the unemployed movement had receded even in the minds of its activists, as war became more and more likely. Both Wal Hannington and Harry McShane end their accounts of the NUWM's history at this point.[47] Yet they leave their readers with a false impression through what amounts almost to a conspiracy of silence. For the movement lived on.

Notes

1 NAC *Report*, 9-10 February 1935, 25-6 May 1935. Circular D/49, 7 March 1935 (WH/CP/A2a).
2 Ibid., 9-10 February 1935.
3 HQ *Newsletter*, nos. 1, 4 1935 (WH/CP/A2c). *Unemployed Leader*, June 1935.

4 *Unemployed Leader*, June, July 1935.
5 'National Headquarters Repudiates the Line of Lewis Jones', 5 July 1935 (WH/CP/A2d).
6 Phil Abrahams and George Brown, typescript n.d., South Wales Miners' Library. On the problems of relations between the SWMF and the NUWM, see the letter of 4 November 1934 from J.S. Williams of Dowlais to a SWMF lodge (A/i/3) making out his case because of the refusal of lodge officers to accept his contributions, and CPGB South Wales District to J.S. Williams (B/ii/2) accepting that the nomination of a SWMF member as secretary of a NUWM District Council would lead to a fight to prevent him from being expelled from the SWMF (J.S. Williams papers, South Wales Coalfield Archive).
7 H. Pollitt, *Forward!* London 1936, p.12 (Maitland-Sara Collection).
8 CP: *Report* of the Central Committee to the 15th Party Congress, 16-19 September, 1938, pp.36-7 (Maitland-Sara Collection).
9 Undated letter from Northampton branch NUWM to Northampton Trades Council (Northants Record Office).
10 HQ Newsletter no.14, 1935 (WH/CP/A2c).
11 'Statement for Discussion at Meetings of Courts of Referees and Appeal Tribunal Representatives' (WH/CP/A2e).
12 NAC *Report*, 9-10 February 1935, p.1.
13 'Draft Resolution on Tasks', for meeting on 28-9 September 1935 (WH/CP/A2d).
14 'To All Branches, DCs. Lies Used to Defeat the Unity of Employed and Unemployed' (WH/CP/A2d).
15 Quoted by S.Shaw, op.cit., p.319.
16 Kingsford, op.cit.,p.209.
17 *Reading Evening Gazette*, 3 November 1936.
18 E. Wilkinson. *The Town That Was Murdered*, London 1939, p.209.
19 Interview with the late John Jackson, 8 July 1983.
20 B.D. Vernon, *Ellen Wilkinson*, London 1982, p.145.
21 *Manchester Guardian*, 13 November 1936.
22 See Ben Pimlott in the *Guardian*, 21 July 1986, for example.
23 'HQ in Serious Financial Difficulties'. Circulars D92, 93 (WH/CP/A2d).
24 R.Croucher, *Engineers At War*, London 1982, pp.34-5.
25 McShane and Smith, op.cit., p.219.
26 NAC *Report* 4-5 July 1936, pp.4-5.
27 Ibid.
28 Ibid, 28-9 November 1936, p.6.
29 Undated newspaper cutting in WH/CP. Interview of Winnie Hannington by Doug Low (date unknown).
30 NAC *Report*, 29-30 August 1936.
31 'Explanation re Vote on War Resolution' (WH/CP/A2e). *Resolutions* Passed at the Tenth National Conference, p.3.
32 *Resolutions* Passed at the Tenth National Conference, p.3.
33 Francis, op.cit., p.192.
34 Kingsford, op.cit., p.225. See also B. Alexander, *British Volunteers for Liberty: Spain 1936-39*, London 1982, pp.34-5.

35 *Resolutions* Passed at the Tenth National Conference, pp.13-14. *Daily Worker*, 23 January 1937.
36 NUWM, *The Hawick Scheme: Woollen Goods for Spain*, London 1937.
37 Ibid.
38 Ibid.
39 Letter to Headquarters, 28 June 1939 (WH/MML/A.VII.1B).
40 H. Birkett to Headquarters, 21 August 1939 (WH/MML/A.VII.1B).
41 *Resolutions* Passed at the Tenth National Conference.
42 *News Review*, 5 January 1939.
43 Ibid. *Daily Telegraph*, 30 December 1938. *Picture Post*, February 1939.
44 *Daily Worker*, 24 March 1939.
45 H. Davies, *The Lean Years. Unemployed Struggles and the NUWM in Nottingham*, Middlesbrough 1984, pp.33-8.
46 Interview with Tom McKay, 2 January 1987.
47 *Never On Our Knees*, pp.328-9. McShane and Smith, op.cit., p.233.

9

Final Struggles and an Indecent Burial, 1939-46

Suspension

The headquarters committee met on 2 September 1939 to consider the NUWM's future given the clear imminence of war with Germany. The outcome of its deliberations was communicated soon afterwards to branches. The circular began by celebrating the achievements of the unemployed movement, and went on to argue that all of the significant gains made by the unemployed since 1920 had been won as a result of the movement's work. The NUWM, then, had made a valuable contribution and was still a substantial asset to the labour movement as a whole. But the committee recognised that this activity had been carried out in the context of mass unemployment, and that during a war, 'There will be no mass unemployment in the sense that provides the basis for a movement like the NUWM.'[1] Given that the NUWM's human resources remained an asset, yet there was no real basis for mass work, the committee reported that the NAC had decided on a novel solution. The NUWM was to be 'suspended' in such a way as to maintain existing contacts and channels of communication so that the movement could be rebuilt as soon as large-scale unemployment reappeared. This suspension was justified in the following terms:

> We use the term 'suspend' deliberately, because we are certain that whether the war is of short or long duration, under capitalism the problem of mass unemployment will immediately arise again on the termination of hostilities, and that in all probability such unemployment will be more extensive and acute than that which followed the Armistice of 1918.[2]

District Councils and branches were instructed to call meetings to explain the precise nature of the decision and its consequences to members and to devise ways of retaining contacts and of keeping alive the movement's spirit so that the NUWM would be in a position to revive itself when peace came.[3]

The NAC had decided, on the basis of its Marxist analysis, that unemployment would inevitably reappear, and to put the NUWM into a sort of cold storage. The great merit of their decision was to recognise the possibility of having to revive the movement after the war. But there were problems, too, with the policy. The form which was decided upon rested on the maintenance of a London headquarters office with a paid official, supported by trade union donations and reserves held by branches. The task of headquarters was defined as helping those who remained unemployed, and giving advice on dependants' allowances to servicemen's wives.[4] But these jobs could also be carried out by branches, which now had practically no funds with which to work. If the aim was to maintain contacts locally, this might have been better achieved by emphasising the branches rather than the centre. Moreover, there was now little possibility of anyone except headquarters affecting the direction of the rump organisation.

For the first two years of the war, the NUWM's remaining activists found a role of sorts. Unemployment proved remarkably persistent, and there were still some 200,000 out of work as late as July 1941, when the Germans invaded the Soviet Union. Many of the unemployed were concentrated in the mining regions which had been the movement's strongholds. The political will to work amongst the unemployed was also present in the Communist Party which at this time was opposing the war. In its key policy document for 1940, *The Communist Party in Wartime*, the party's leadership asserted that 'unemployment remains one of our outstanding social problems, and it is most essential that organisation and activity among the unemployed should be developed without delay'.[5] Seen in this context, the 'suspension' appeared to take on a new and more active meaning.

The branches were playing the role of community representation and advocacy in circumstances in which people's lives were subject to constant disruption. They

therefore found a niche which was wider than that provided
by the registered unemployed alone, and were forced by
circumstances to take a wider view and to become an advice
and representation agency for the unwaged. The movement
was also building new branches. In September 1940, a new
branch was formed in Southampton to deal with the problems
of unemployed dockers; soon afterwards, contact was made
with people wishing to establish a new branch in Northern
Ireland.[6] The distribution of branches and the nature of their
work was reported in a circular of March 1942, which stated
that there were functioning branches in Lanarkshire,
Nottinghamshire, Durham and Cornwall, which were dealing
with issues relating to pensions, service wives' allowances and
so on.[7]

The movement's final crisis was precipitated by the
disappearance of personnel at the centre, rather than in the
branches. Given its structure, the organisation could afford to
suffer the loss of many branches, but not the loss of its
headquarters. Until early July 1940, Hannington had still
been giving advice and signing circulars, but by the end of that
month he was receiving written reports from the new 'General
Secretary', the previously obscure Eric Edney.[8] Edney took his
rather precarious position very seriously. He fought a losing
battle with commendable tenacity but insufficient realism.
His reports to Hannington were a catalogue of national
stalwarts who were no longer willing or able to continue their
activity. Don Renton had been working as an organiser until
the autumn of 1940, but had ended his involvement before
1941. Soon afterwards, Edney complained to Hannington that
'It is remarkable how people drop out of the movement like a
stone – Jimmy Ancrum, Harry McShane, Mary, now
Don ...'[9] By February 1941, Edney felt he had cause to
complain that Hannington was not writing to him sufficiently
regularly. In March 1942, he reported to branches that
Hannington could no longer play any part in the NUWM as
he had been elected National Organiser for the AEU.
Hannington had been working as a toolmaker since the
summer of 1940, and was well able to capitalise on his
reputation within the engineering union to obtain his
prestigious position by national election. Edney reminded
members that the NUWM had initially sprung from the shop

stewards' movement in engineering, and pointed out that 'Now the wheel has turned', with the NUWM giving strength to the engineers.[10] Edney's grasp of history was firm; now he himself had to bow to its logic. During 1941, he had been called up to the forces, and despite arguing that he was exempt from call-up because he was a full-time trade union official, was compelled to recognise defeat by March 1942.[11] The movement now had no headquarters staff, and a decision had to be taken about its future.

Even at this point there was no rush to finally bury the NUWM. It was not until the end of April 1943 that a special meeting of the headquarters committee was called. This meeting produced a memorandum which was very similar in its text to that of September 1939. In fact, it was exactly the same in its argument. Only the conclusions were different. In a new closing paragraph, the memorandum gave an indication of why the committee now felt that the NUWM should be wound up:

> We are of the opinion that in the event of mass unemployment recurring after the war it will become a matter for concern for the entire working class movement in that period to accept responsibility for divising the form of organisation and action necessary to combat it.[12]

At the time when this document was written, the attitude of the Communist Party to the war had changed completely; it was now pushing for full support for the war effort. From being a party which wished to preserve bodies like the NUWM as thorns in the flesh of the capitalist class, the Communist Party had become anxious to be seen as a responsible party with legitimate claims to being a serious electoral proposition. In this situation, organisations like the NUWM were little more than an unfortunate reminder of the immediate past. The context of national politics was also very different. There was full employment, Ernie Bevin was Minister of Labour, and the Beveridge Report had just appeared, recommending a comprehensive new system of welfare. Despite the refusal of the government to implement the Report's recommendations, the whole problem of unemployment appeared both a distant prospect and, to some extent at least, one which the entire movement would shoulder. Yet the committee's contention that, should there be any problems, then they would be the responsibility of the labour movement as a whole, was made in the knowledge that for many years that responsibility had been inadequately discharged. It was an optimistic assertion. The absence of mass unemployment after 1945 could not be predicted in 1943.

The continuation of the NUWM into the war had shown how great the momentum developed in the previous twenty years had been, and how flexible some branches could be as they adapted to entirely new problems. Despite all the forces militating against its survival, the movement refused to die. When the NUWM was finally dissolved, it was a much messier business than either Hannington or McShane cared to recall. With Hannington and Edney gone, the question of whether there was still a role for the NUWM to play in a modified or 'suspended' form was a debatable one. But there was no debate. Communist Party politics no longer allowed the usefulness of the NUWM's continued existence in any form, and what remained of the movement was killed off.

On 14 February 1946, Hannington finally wrote to his old comrade Harry McShane saying that the affairs of the NUWM 'have now at last been completely wound up'. A balance of £32 had remained, of which £7 19s.11d had been paid to 'old Frazer' who had looked after the office, whilst the rest was donated to the 'People's Printing Press' (*sic*), which published the *Daily Worker*. Meticulous to the very end, Hannington asked McShane to keep his copy of the final balance sheet safe, in case it should be needed at a later date.[13] Only then, when full employment was a reality, could he safely wind up the affairs of the organisation for whose creation he had argued and worked so hard more than a quarter of a century earlier.

Notes

1 Memo. of headquarters meeting held 2 September 1939 (WH/CP/A2f).
2 Ibid.
3 Ibid.
4 'Guarantor Plan' (undated circular) (WH/CP/A2f).

5 CP: *The CP in Wartime* (London, 1939), p.17 (Maitland-Sara Collection).
6 Edney to Hannington, 23 September 1940 (WH/CP/A2h).
7 Circular to Branches, 8 March 1942 (WH/CP/A2g).
8 Edney to Hannington, 31 July 1940 (WH/CP/A2h).
9 Edney to Hannington, 4 October 1940 (WH/CP/A2h).
10 Circular to Branches, 8 March 1942 (WH/CP/A2g).
11 Edney to Hannington, 10 March 1942 (WH/CP/A2h).
12 Memo. of National Headquarters Committee Meeting, 24 April 1943 (WH/CP/A2f).
13 Hannington to McShane, 15 February 1946 (WH/CP/A2f).

10

The Achievement of the NUWM

After two decades of unremitting propaganda, agitation and struggle, the unemployed movement was quietly buried. Wal Hannington estimated that around 1,000,000 people had passed through its ranks. What had they achieved? Viewed from the 1980s, perhaps the most obvious achievement lay in the very existence and longevity of the NUW(C)M. The movement had faced enormous difficulties, and yet it had survived in such an active form for so long. Probably the most fundamental problem that it had always to confront was that of how to develop the involvement of those who were not already associated with the labour movement. This derived, of course, from the position of the unemployed as isolated and often demoralised individuals consumed by the desire for work. It was possible to mobilise many people in sporadic actions, but much harder to absorb them into the movement's internal life. At times, notably in the mid-1920s, the NUW(C)M came close to extinction because of the periodic 'slumps' to which this gave rise. It was the commitment of the Communist Party to the NUW(C)M which provided essential scaffolding for the unstable edifice, and the party became increasingly important to the NUW(C)M, supporting and sustaining it from its own human and material resources. Its members brought discipline and centralisation to the unemployed movement, and thereby created a powerful machine and a vital weapon, able to mount major operations like Hunger Marches with great efficiency by the early 1930s. The NUW(C)M, then, owed its very existence to the CPGB. But there was a price to be paid: increasing concentration of power in the hands of its political leaders, who picked their way home none too delicately through changing Communist policies. At its origins, the NUW(C)M had been very open to the influence of its rank and file.[A series of subtle changes concentrated in the mid-1920s preceded a phase in which the Communist-led headquarters dominated the organisation whilst holding off complete control by the Communist King Street officials.] From the mid-1930s, this independence was swiftly eroded.

Centralisation of power in the NUW(C)M had some negative consequences. It reduced opportunities for democratic involvement of the unemployed and the upward flow of creative ideas which had led, for example, to the highly successful Hunger March of 1922-23. It made the task of police spies easier: one spy on the NAC provided the government with a great deal of information. Above all, it restricted the influence of the organisation on those who were reluctant to accept the Communist Party's political direction. Increasingly, it appeared to the outside observer that policies originating in Moscow and CPGB headquarters were being adopted by the unemployed movement irrespective of their appropriateness. Here was an important problem, for the NUW(C)M probably never reached more than 10 per cent of the workless at any given time, and this in turn was why the TUC had been able to repudiate and isolate the movement. Hannington and many other old activists constantly pointed to the bureaucrats' hostility as the major limiting factor on the movement's influence. Apparently it did not occur to them that the internal running of the NUW(C)M had any bearing on the problem. They seem to have regarded the structures and methods adopted to have been entirely necessary and 'natural'. Given the nature of the unemployed, and Communist history, they may well have been right.

Ultimately, however, the movement's nature and evolution are secondary matters. The NUW(C)M's achievement has finally to be judged by what was gained through its fight for improved conditions. Its contemporary critics suggested that nothing had been gained, that the workless had simply been exploited by the Communist Party for its own ends, and that improved benefits, procedures and treatment would have come without protest. In this, they have been followed by some historians, who have often tended to treat the NUWM as little other than an attempt to carry out a revolution led by the unemployed.[1] In these terms, the NUWM obviously failed, because at no time was the leadership either of the NUWM or of the Communist Party of the view that an unemployed movement could achieve any such thing. They always took the view that social change would necessarily be led primarily by the employed working class; this was a central tenet of Communist politics. Other historians simply ignore the NUWM, which remains curiously absent from much of the literature. There are more than a few historical works on Britain in the inter-war years which totally overlook the NUWM, an achievement which comes close to presenting *Hamlet* without the Prince of Denmark.[2] Such writers often invite us to accept the Jarrow marchers as a symbol of unemployed activity in the inter-war years. Hannington himself scornfully and correctly rejected all of these arguments and approaches. Now, in a new period of mass unemployment, it seems particularly appropriate to revisit the debate and examine the arguments.

One way of measuring the achievement of the NUWM is by measuring it against the aims and hopes of those who joined it. What had *they* hoped to achieve? This is a question which cannot be answered entirely satisfactorily: there were probably as many motives as there were individuals involved. But when old activists were asked, they often referred to the need to improve the levels of benefits and the nature of their treatment. Some referred to NUWM activity as a logical outcome of their situation as unemployed Communists. A few, like John Jackson of Birkenhead or Mr Hudson of Bradford, came from religious backgrounds and saw unemployment as immoral, something which could not be passively tolerated by any right-thinking human being. Perhaps the best and most succinct summary of the motivations of the 'average' member has been offered by Sid Elias:

> I think that what people hoped to achieve was first of all the elimination of procedures by the bureaucrats which deprived them of what little benefits were obtainable in those days; and secondly, to try and improve the benefits; and thirdly to impress upon the government or authorities or whoever they were the question of how they could provide us with work. I don't think there were any revolutionary aims attached to the unemployed workers' movement.[3]

Elias's summary seems a fair one which is worth accepting as a yardstick.

As far as the first aim mentioned by Elias is concerned, there can be little doubt that the procedures were to some extent improved over the inter-war years. Simply by helping to remove the Guardians, the NUWM helped to improve the procedures. The Guardians had always viewed their work as essentially charitable, and as a defence of the rates. The PACs and the UAB, although obviously not profligate organisations, worked to a much more uniform set of rules which to some extent at least recognised the rights of claimants. Also, unlike the Guardians, the national procedures established the rights of representation and appeal. Elias himself referred to an improvement in people's treatment being apparent from the late 1920s, and this would certainly coincide with these changes. In addition, recent historians of these procedures have contended that the regulations underwent a slow but perceptible process of relaxation as time went on, probably as a result of argument through representation.[4] Although the system was still experienced as harsh and inequitable, it was certainly the case that some of the worst horrors of the Poor Law had been removed by 1939. The improvement was certainly neither dramatic nor universal, but there were those who felt that it could be detected.

What effect had the NUWM's agitation had on the level of benefits? The movement constantly agitated for increases in both insurance and non-contributory benefits, and this agitation did bring some improvement in insurance benefit. Economic historians agree that the relationship between benefits and earnings improved from benefits standing at 40 per cent of average wages in 1924 to 60 per cent in 1938.[5] This level of income was generally insufficient to keep people above Rowntree's poverty line, even at the 1938 level.[6] But the transference of large numbers of unemployed into the non-contributory sector in the early 1930s, and their subjection to the hated Family Means Test brought considerable cuts in living standards for many. Clearly, the position of people in this position could hardly be said to have 'improved' in any material sense. The NUWM was generally in the position, not of forcing improvements, but of fighting off cuts, especially in the 1930s. The position of the unemployed in the non-contributory sector was to some extent protected, but not improved, by the NUWM. Yet there is a perspective in which the position was bettered, if one compares pre-1914 and post-1924 conditions. Before 1914, a larger proportion of the workless was being forced into the workhouse. By the late 1920s, the workhouse had been pushed well to the margins of public thought and discussion about unemployment, whilst out-relief and mass insurance schemes had become accepted as a better way of dealing with the problem. In this sense, some gains had been made, although given the general level of destitution, the unemployed themselves could have been forgiven for failing to notice it. What credit could be claimed by the NUWM for these changes? Very often, the argument has been made out that the NUWM had little or nothing to do with them, and that they would have come anyway as a result of government policy. The burden of proof surely rests with those who make such counter-factual assertions. The fact is that the NUWM did mobilise hundreds of thousands of people in large-scale protests, which in almost every case led to some improvement in government proposals, generally announced at some time after the decision to organise a Hunger March had been made public. To ignore the timing of these concessions, or to refuse to acknowledge them as such, is to turn a blind eye to chronology, to do violence to the historical record and to insult the intelligence of the reader.

There is another aspect to the question of the level of benefits, which has to do with the money which people actually received as opposed to the dole's theoretical level. The NUWM fought thousands of cases, which were frequently disqualifications by which the claimant was driven to dependence on his or her family, destitution and sometimes even suicide. Large numbers of people were saved from these fates who would otherwise have had to accept the diktat of cost-cutting officials.

Finally, the NUWM had helped to protect the earnings levels of industrial workers. For various reasons which economic historians have pointed out, governments were concerned in these years to ensure that benefits did not become too 'high' in relation to earnings. It has been suggested by Brian Sadler, for example, that it was mainly earnings that determined benefits.[7] If this was the case, there can be no doubt that the NUWM made an indirect contribution to benefits by helping wage rates to be maintained. The NUWM's constant support for trade unionists in action on picket lines could only have been of positive assistance in preserving bargaining power and therefore keeping earnings up. The NUWM provided a surrogate for militant trade unionism which helped both employed and unemployed.

Sid Elias also gave as one of the reasons for people joining the movement a desire to impress on the authorities the need to provide work. The main effects of the movement's activities in this direction were probably located in the post-1945 period. Major job creation schemes had not been a feature of the inter-war years, but the movement had certainly impressed many people, including Beveridge, with the force of its arguments concerning the damaging effects of unemployment on the economy, society and the individual. By the time Beveridge presented his famous report in 1943, most politicians recognised the need to pay attention to the popular demand for full employment at the end of the war. It was principally the Labour Party that benefited from this consensus, but it had been the extra-parliamentary activity of the NUWM that had made the human problems of unemployment visible to the public eye in a way that no parliamentary orator could hope to emulate. Between the wars, the NUWM ensured that the failure of governments to provide either work or adequate maintenance was publicly made painfully apparent. The emaciated evidence was constantly marching up and down before the nation's eyes. The NUWM had contributed to the formation of a national consensus that reconstruction after the Second World War should lead to full employment. The NUWM had been as effective in this direction as leading trade unionists and Labour politicians like Bevin. While Bevin produced numerous interesting blueprints for major employment projects, and probably had some positive effect on public opinion by doing so, there was no shortage of people with Keynesian-style ideas on how public funds should be spent. The central question was whether it made sense to spend money in this way at all. The NUWM reminded people of the human cost of unemployment in a way which supported the arguments for doing so far more eloquently than any number of fiscal estimates or projections.

Wal Hannington made another claim for the work of the NUWM which merits examination. In *Unemployed Struggles*, and then again more firmly in *Never On Our Knees*, he argued that the unemployed movement had played a central role in preventing fascism from developing as a major force in Britain. The argument did not rest solely on the movement's open anti-fascist activities in the late 1930s, but on a deeper contention that the unemployed had, thanks to their Communist leadership, set the political agenda in non-fascist terms. If this was so, then the whole of British society would owe the NUWM a huge debt for saving it from such a nightmare. Hannington's case has some substance. The NUWM did indeed set the political agenda among the unemployed in the way that he suggested, even though it only touched the active minority among the workless. The British unemployed, whose German counterparts had been an important source of support for the Nazis, were not especially taken by the politics of Mosley and the British Union of Fascists. But it is important to set Hannington's argument in a wider context. It thereby becomes less impressive, because the depth of the inter-war crisis in Britain did not approach that in Weimar Germany. The humiliating terms of the Versailles settlement at the end of the First World War, and the fragility of Weimar's social and political support, had no parallel in Britain. Britain's rulers had a political authority that could only be wondered at by German politicians before 1933.

Hannington made one further claim for the NUWM, which had to do with its creation of opportunities for activism within a broad labour movement framework. The movement urged people to do something rather than starve in silence, to fight for the right to live. It was better to do something about your situation than to accept it passively. What did you have to lose? To participate in a march or demonstration or represent someone was an achievement of sorts, which implicitly refuted the charge that you were unemployed because you were lazy and unenterprising. Through this, you could recover your dignity and self-respect as a human being. Above all, the movement stressed collective activity, which took people out of that corrosive isolation which sapped the confidence of the workless so badly. All of this could easily be dismissed by critics: what point was there to such activism? Hannington argued that the point was that demoralisation would have been even worse among the unemployed had it not been for the existence of the NUWM. By demoralisation, he meant the individual blaming him or herself for being unemployed. For him, it had been healthy that some at least had refused to blame themselves as individuals for a social evil. That way lay psychological ill health and suicide. It is difficult to disagree with this argument; the testimony of old militants bears witness to the fact that the lives of many were enriched by participation in the movement. Many found themselves there.

Hannington's argument could be taken further, and applied to the health of the labour movement as a whole. The NUWM played an important part in reproducing the potential leaders available to working class organisations. While the trade unions were tiny, dormant organisations, and the Labour Party offered mainly electoral activity, the NUWM presented a wide range of opportunities for people to develop as activists. We hope that we have shown that the NUWM was not simply a marching organisation; the great diversity of its work created a school with a wide curriculum. Many militants used their training to become shop stewards or lay officials in the following decade. The same point can be seen in another way, as Bas Barker (who had been active in the Chesterfield branch) pointed out. The unemployed movement kept the extra-parliamentary tradition alive in the labour movement in the difficult decade between the defeat of the General Strike and the resurgence of the trade unions in the late 1930s. In this period, it was the public presence of the labour movement.

Measured in terms of the aims of those who had joined the NUWM, then, there were undoubtedly major successes to record. In a general sense, they created the political climate within which Labour could make rapid electoral progress as the party of welfare. At the same time they laid the foundations of a new system of relief, traditionally credited solely to Beveridge and dubbed 'the Welfare State'. Beveridge himself was disappointed at the way his ideas were implemented, as well he might have been. Nevertheless, the

'Welfare State' was much less humiliating in practice than being on the parish. It is hard to conceive of this having happened without the work of the NUWM. The Guardians were abolished largely because of the pressure put on them by the unemployed movement, well before the Beveridge Report. Moreover, the right to representation within the system unquestionably came from the NUWM's persistent advocacy and practice of that right between the wars. Indeed, Beveridge himself recognised the contribution of the NUWM, who had helped him shape a more human vision of the way that people who had fallen out of work should be treated.

In many ways, then, as it recognised at the time, the unemployed movement fought not so much for its benefit as for that of future generations. These benefits, such as they are, are again under attack today, and it is the clear responsibility of the present generation, whether in or out of work, to defend what their predecessors fought for. In fact, our task is not simply to defend these achievements, but to assist in creating a society in which, as Wal Hannington put it, unemployment is no more than an evil memory of the past.

Notes

1 M. Bruce, *The Coming of the Welfare State,* London 1961, p.266.
2 See, for example, T.O. Lloyd, *Empire to Welfare State, English History 1900-76,* Oxford 1978, E.E. Reynolds and N.H. Brasher, *Britain in the Twentieth Century, 1900-64,* Cambridge 1966 or D. Thompson (with additional material by G. Warner), *England in the Twentieth Century, 1914-79,* London 1981. None of these well known overviews contains a single line about the NUWM.
3 J. Halstead, R. Harrison, J. Stevenson, op.cit., p.41.
4 B. Sadler, 'Unemployment and Unemployment Benefits in Twentieth Century Britain: A Lesson of the Thirties', in K. Cowling et al, *Out Of Work,* Coventry,1984, p.19.
5 Sadler, op.cit., p.28.
6 Ibid.
7 Ibid.

Index